To Richard & Lisa,
   To enjoy for your new adventure into
 a holiday home - have fun.
                          With Love,
                          Sue, Gerry,
                          Oliver, Freddie.
                          & William

                          xxx

                          Xmas '06

HOME
essentials

HOME
essentials

hundreds of inspirational ideas for
decorating and furnishing your home

RYLAND

PETERS

& SMALL

LONDON NEW YORK

First published in the UK in 2006 by
Ryland Peters & Small
20–21 Jockey's Fields
London WC1R 4BW
www.rylandpeters.com

10 9 8 7 6 5 4 3 2 1

ISBN-10: 1-84597-265-1
ISBN-13: 978-1-84597-265-3

Text copyright © Ros Byam Shaw,
Maggie Stevenson, Fay Sweet,
Judith Wilson and Ryland Peters
& Small 2003, 2004, 2006
Design and photographs copyright
© Ryland Peters & Small 2006

This book was originally published
in separate volumes:
Living Room Essentials, *Kitchen
Essentials*, *Bathroom Essentials*,
Bedroom Essentials and
Children's Room Essentials.

The authors' moral rights have
been asserted.

A CIP record for this book is
available from the British Library.

Printed and bound in China.

Senior designer Catherine Griffin
Senior editor Henrietta Heald
Picture research Emily Westlake
Production Eleanor Cant
Art director Anne-Marie Bulat
Publishing director Alison Starling

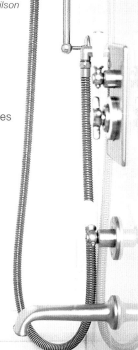

contents

only the essentials

See how decorative planning works in action, with the help of abundant colour photographs of real homes. Whether you are planning a total revamp of your living space or are looking for fresh ideas for a particular room, this book will be your indispensable companion.

Decorating and furnishing a home, large or small, can be a daunting prospect, especially if you are starting from scratch. From kitchen appliances to bedroom window treatments, there are a multitude of choices to be made – and endless decisions to be taken about how to arrange the various spaces for maximum comfort and efficiency. Visiting a bathroom showroom, for example, may prove to be an overwhelming experience if you don't know exactly what you are looking for.

Home Essentials will be your invaluable guide through the maze of home design and decoration. This information-packed book aims to give you all the inspiration and advice you need to create the home of your dreams – without getting sidetracked by fussy details or complicated schemes.

Leading interiors writers Ros Byam Shaw, Maggie Stevenson, Fay Sweet and Judith Wilson offer you the fruits of their combined knowledge and experience. They take you on a tour of the home, from Living Rooms to Cooking & Eating Spaces, from Bedrooms to Bathrooms, reviewing the basic components of each room – from colour to storage and display – before moving on to explore the style options for each space. The showcased looks include Contemporary, Country, Retro and Family-friendly, and there are features on getting the best use from compact rooms.

Home Essentials gives you only what you need to make the most of your living space – and turn a potential burden into a pleasure.

living rooms

elements

planning the space

For the lucky few, the living room is a tranquil space for winding down and a cool style statement in terms of objects and furniture. But, for most people, it is the nerve centre of the home, where family life, socializing and television-watching coexist, day in, day out. The living room is a harder-working room than most of us realize, so begin by asking yourself some salient questions. How much time will be spent there, and what activities will go on there? What favourite possessions do you want to show off? What needs to be stored? Can the room be rearranged for entertaining?

Far left Even a subtle shift in furniture style or colour – plastics versus leather, primaries contrasted with neutrals – can separate areas without compromising the spirit of an open-plan living space.

Left In a narrow living room, several upholstered dining chairs, rather than bulky armchairs, provide casual seating without cluttering the space.

Above and below Add essential intimacy to a large living area by grouping chairs and sofas in a sociable cluster.

- The living room is probably the hardest-working room in your home; **make a list** of all the functions you require of it.

- For **careful space management**, draw up a plan of your room and cut out **scale shapes** to represent your furnishings.

- A real or real-effect fire creates a **natural focal point** and is always worth the investment.

- Decide **at the start** where the sound system, television and **other equipment** will go so that they can be housed both practically and tidily.

Left and far left Dual-purpose furnishings – a coffee table with drawers, cupboards which offer display and storage – help a room design to work harder. **Right** If space is limited, you can create optical illusions with slim, 'barely there' furniture. **Below right** In an open-plan space, a table behind the sofa provides a visual and practical division of zones.

The correct arrangement of furniture is crucial in a living room. Careful planning will mean that you can watch television in comfort, chat easily with friends, and may even be able to squeeze in enough room for a separate seating area for quiet reading or card games. A natural focal point in the room – be it a fireplace or a wonderful outdoor view – can be a useful decorative starting point.

Draw a scale plan of the room, cut out to-scale shapes of existing furniture and experiment with different layouts. In terms of human traffic flow, space between furniture always seems less once translated into three dimensions, so err on the generous side.

Good lighting can make or break a living room. If possible, replace central pendant lighting, which casts ugly shadows. But don't do away with overhead lighting altogether – every living room needs the option of bright light sometimes – and don't forget task lights for reading. Plan for plenty of side lights, too, and put all lights on dimmer switches.

Controlling natural light is equally important. If sunlight is too dazzling, consider screening it with shutters or blinds. If the room is naturally shady, place at least one chair and table next to a window to capitalize on daylight.

colour schemes

When choosing colours for your living room, go classic. A neutral colour scheme offers the best backdrop for attractive possessions, furnishings and artworks, and is easily updated with fresh splashes of colour. In addition, it diverts attention from an obvious trend or date of furniture. A wing chair in dark paisley may be described as 'period', whereas the same chair upholstered in white cotton is simply a pretty shape that blends easily with other styles in the room.

Left Cheap ready-made curtains are a wonderful way to ring the changes in a room by adding new colour. If choosing sheers, bear in mind that strong sunlight will dilute even the brightest of shades.

Above Spray-painted doors create a sleek, professional finish, showing how the most utilitarian of storage pieces, from a simple cabinet to built-in units, can be transformed into a colour statement.

Far left and right Focus attention on a bright artwork by keeping the rest of the room quietly neutral. Even a plain painted artist's canvas can be used to 'lift' a tired scheme, adding fresh colours each season.

Choose upholstery in cool tones, from white to deep graphite, and furniture in wood, metal or rattan. Then apply this palette to smaller items, from ceramic lamp bases to stone platters, glass vases and oak photograph frames. If there are wooden floorboards, consider sisal, jute or neutral-coloured wool rugs.

Now you are ready to bring colour and pattern into play. Whether it's a single large piece, like an armchair upholstered in tangerine denim, or several smaller items, such as shell-pink side tables, the point to remember is that the colours should be easy and inexpensive to change. Look out for sale-bargain fabrics or furniture that can be repainted. If a patterned or coloured piece is to last, make sure you love it in its own right as opposed to tying it into a complete coordinated scheme. One armchair upholstered in green chintz will look good with a white sofa, or – five years on – with a grey one; it is only when the chintz has been matched to other elements, such as chairs and curtains, that problems arise.

We don't all want to live in a neutral space, so if you love colour then put it on the walls. Remember that your chosen shades will deeply affect the room's ambience: off-pastels are soothing; bright blocks stimulating; and deep, sombre tones sophisticated yet warm. As your sitting room is the chief

Top Lift plain upholstery with detailing such as buttoning or a contrast piping.
Above A bright, generous throw is a useful trick for adding instant colour to a tired sofa, although its informality works best in a more traditional setting.
Right Choosing to upholster a single piece in a bright shade may seem self-indulgent, but it adds a novel twist to an otherwise classic scheme.
Far right Plan coloured upholstery with imagination. A piece needn't always be all one colour. Find a creative upholsterer and ask for mix-and-match two-tone plains for a truly individual look.

Above left Dark wood panelling creates a sophisticated background for bright flashes of upholstery.

Above A multicoloured rug allows you to pick out key tones in upholstery or accessories.

Far left Leather comes in a surprisingly varied choice of colours, from pastels to brights.

Left A 'wardrobe' of cushions can be used to change a neutral scheme each season.

- Wall **texture radically affects colour** – matt paint or wool-felt walling will deepen a shade, whereas eggshell or sparkly papers will lighten it.

- **Create a colour board** – complete with fabric, paint and flooring samples – and examine it in different lights.

- Colours need not match exactly; it is more crucial to **get the tonal balance right.**

- **Think big** – paint huge boards or borrow large fabric samples to get the full effect of a hue, rather than relying on tiny chips and swatches.

entertaining space – and a design statement for visitors – be a little more daring. If it is a room that is used primarily by night, choose dramatic colours that look good in artificial light. Picking elegant pastels, by contrast, will deliberately set apart a more formal living room from a family den.

Even braver is to put blocks of colour onto the floor or as window treatments. It gives a chic, well-coordinated look, although the disadvantage is that if you tire of the colour it's an expensive mistake to rectify. So be realistic. Pale, light-reflecting floor shades are tempting, but will require constant cleaning, whereas a vivid colour may 'fight' with other possessions, making it necessary to edit favourite things. Many interior designers stick to the golden rule of choosing only earth colours for the floor, from green to ochre, never an unnatural sky blue. Remember, too, that strong-coloured curtains will create a disruptive contrasting block against the walls. Choosing both in the same shade is more soothing.

Above left Wall colour does not have to be uniform. Bands of graded colour, passing from dark to light, create a particularly dramatic effect.

Left In a naturally dark room or a space that is mostly used at night, pick stronger, muted colours that look effective in dim light. Plum, graphite and moss green are good choices.

Opposite In an all-white interior, a splash of colour, in the form of a fabric pattern or painting, looks striking. Here, the harsh contrast is softened by choosing curvy, rather than straight, outlines for the furniture.

Above Keep a lookout for finishes that will improve with age – leather, plaster moulding, gilding, foxed mirrors and antique wood are all good choices.

Left Often the most interesting living rooms result from a combination of styles and materials. But, if you are nervous about mixing disparate pieces, try to pick a theme. Lots of furniture with skinny legs, for example, looks funky and fun. Alternatively, try all curved pieces together, or a preponderance of boxy silhouettes.

furniture &
soft furnishings

Choosing a style for the furnishing of your living room is the exciting part, but pay close attention to your budget. A living room demands investment pieces, from sofas to bookshelves, not to mention metres of fabric and the almost ruinous cost of making up soft furnishings. It can be an expensive business, so try to compose a classic scheme that will endure and can be updated with trendier accessories.

This page Newly fashionable, the modular sofa has certain benefits. If your budget is tight, buying a combination of stool, daybed and corner pieces could be more cost-effective than a conventional sofa plus two armchairs. Wonderful for small spaces, because of its streamlined outline, it is also one of the most relaxed seating options available, perfect both for socializing and sprawling.

Left When choosing furniture styles, think carefully about how you use the living room. Do you prefer to sit up and chat or to chill out horizontally? If the latter, a daybed or long, lean sofa is indispensable, as are armchairs with angled backs. Never be afraid to try out furniture in the shop, since this is the only way to be sure of achieving comfort.

Below If you prefer over-stuffed upholstery and plump cushions, pick a sofa with a sufficiently deep seat, so there is room for both you and the cushions.

The first step in selecting your furnishings is to look at what you have. A sofa can be reupholstered in a new fabric, or a battered side table given a new, distressed paint finish. Ask yourself pertinent questions in order to refine your needs. If you entertain frequently, would two small sofas be better than one large model? Might a daybed suit the room more than an armchair? And a coffee table isn't a necessity if four small side tables will do the job just as well. Think, too, about the practicality and quality of each piece you choose. Although the living room may be used only during evenings or at weekends, its major components need to last at least a decade. So buy the best you can afford, and put your money into the most heavily used pieces. The main sofa should have coil-sprung

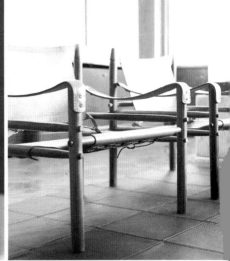

Above left It is easy to focus on major furniture choices, but pay due attention to the smaller items, from side tables to lamps. Ensure that they are practical as well as good-looking.

Above, centre and right However plain your chosen look, it is fun to add zest with unusually styled upholstery or soft furnishings. Good options are contrast stitching or simple borders on cushions, and lacing, studding or buttoning on upholstered items.

Below For a streamlined look, choose pieces that are on a similar level to each other; low-slung sofas demand equally low storage cabinets.

seats and duck-feather-filled cushions, but you could go for foam upholstery on an occasional armchair. There is nothing wrong with veneered wood furniture, but check the quality because some cheap veneers are very fragile. If possible, choose solid wood for a table that will see lots of use. Opt for real metals instead of a metal-effect finish, which may chip.

The key to choosing successful furnishings is versatility. Any of the major pieces will involve a substantial outlay, even a high-street sofa, so you need to be confident that when, in five years' time, the walls are repainted another colour, the furniture will still be going strong, even though small details may need tweaking. It is therefore important to pick designs that can reflect fresh looks. Choose sofas with pretty legs and

an elegant silhouette, giving you the option of choosing plump upholstery or loose covers. Simple, inexpensive MDF or wood pieces can be repainted in different colours. And think of smaller items – console tables or a side chair – as the equivalents of those skirts and trousers that mix and match with the key suit jacket. If attractive in their own right, they can also be moved around the house for visual variety.

In terms of design, there are certain failsafe styles for the sitting room. For upholstery, many classics are still the best. You can't go far wrong with the wing chair or, for a more modern look, a boxy sofa, both of which not only boast a great outline but also look good with antique or contemporary pieces. Ignore clumsy or overly fussy designs with puffy cushions. When choosing tables or cabinets, stick to simple styling in quality materials, and mix curvy and rectangular shapes together. However, don't get hung up on classics at the expense of indulging your personal style. Let that shine through in one or two unusual pieces.

- A living room demands **investment pieces**, so go for a classic scheme that will last – thereby spreading the cost.

- **Dual-purpose furniture**, such as a coffee table with drawers or a dining-cum-work table, helps a living room to work harder.

- **Luxurious upholstery** that also wears well includes wool mixes, linen and chenille. Save silk, satin or suede for occasional chairs.

- Cover cushions or a small chair in **a fabric you adore** – it will look almost as good as an entire sofa upholstered in the fabric, but is much **less expensive**.

Opposite Opting for 'classic' furniture may mean that you end up with a room that looks as though it could belong to your parents. Stay true to your style, but add sophisticated touches. If you like beanbags, for example, pick them in vinyl or leather. Fans of shabby chic might choose a distressed antique mirror rather than a newly gilded one. Whatever your style, make sure that you have cushions you love.

This page Fresh upholstery can transform a second-hand sofa or armchair. Pick neutrals to team with pretty cushions, or a patterned fabric to turn a chair into a strong focal point.

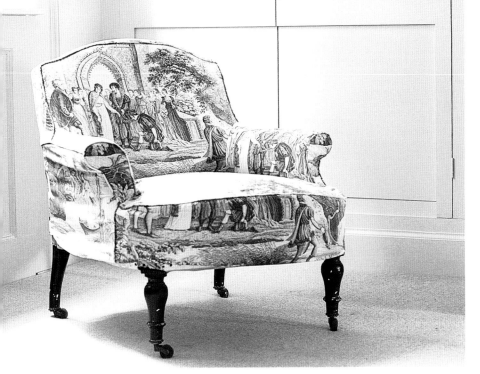

This page Choose translucent blinds in a sunny room to encourage dramatic light-play, as well as to screen rays. Plain blinds, pierced with holes, create particularly pretty effects.
Opposite, left A Roman blind, with its flat panel, is one of the best ways to show off patterned fabric at windows. Lined blinds hang better than unlined ones and prevent show-through from fittings on the back.
Opposite, right A fitted sheer panel hides an ugly view more decoratively than net curtains.

window treatments

The perfect window treatment needs to be functional as well as looking stylish. A good curtain or blind will filter strong sunlight, provide privacy, even protect against chills, not to mention screening a less than enviable urban view. At the same time, a window treatment offers myriad decorative opportunities. It can become a focal point in the absence of an architecturally interesting window frame, highlight a lovely view, or show off a beautiful fabric.

When deciding on window treatments, take account of the shape and size of the windows, the light flow and the view. Consider, too, whether blinds or curtains would be preferable. In general, blinds fit well in a contemporary setting, yet they can be equally appropriate in a traditional room, especially if they are made from heavy linen, damask or a pretty floral. Be imaginative with trims. Look for unusual pulls, from leather thongs to ceramic pebbles, and consider contrasting borders.

However contemporary the mood elsewhere in your home, many people still prefer the softer look and enveloping feel of curtains in a living room. The modern preference is for curtains that fall in strong, sculptural folds and hang from simple poles, never from fussy pelmets.

When planning window treatments, remember that the cost of fabric can really mount up. Interior designers recommend using a cheaper fabric and getting curtains well made, rather than vice versa. Think about lining options. Interlining gives a particularly good drape and is a sensible choice if you live in a chilly clime. If you like the unlined look but need privacy, the ideal compromise is to team unlined curtains with roller blinds.

Above Minimal window treatments, such as discreet shutters, are ideal if you like to watch the world go by.
Below left Investigate unusual curtain hangings, from stringing and eyelets to threading on suspension wires.
Below centre Plain contemporary curtains can be given a decorative twist with an inset panel, pin-tucked detail or a contrast leading edge.
Below right and opposite If privacy isn't an issue, use unlined sheers in plains or patterns to diffuse sunlight.

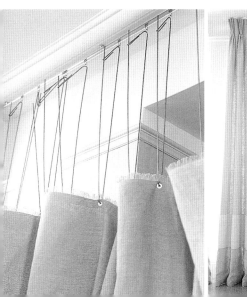

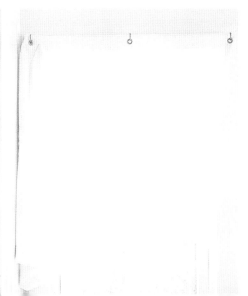

- **Contrast linings**, from plain colours to tiny floral prints, give a decorative boost to plain curtains as well as looking pretty from outside.

- **Curtains need not be permanent.** Use a plain pole fitted with curtain clips as the basis for a regularly changing display, ranging from bright sari lengths to an antique linen tablecloth.

- Don't overlook ready-made **high-street options**. There may be a big price difference between these and custom-made curtains or blinds.

- Dress curtains with plain roller blinds will **save on the amount of fabric required**.

storage & display

However busy it becomes in reality, the living room should have the potential to look tranquil and tidy. That is why efficient storage is so important. Before deciding on storage styles, think long and hard about what really needs to be stored in the living room. Depending on the size of your home, it may be possible to relocate certain items – old photos or out-of-favour CDs – to the attic or basement. If space is tight, have regular clearouts. Things you keep in the living room should be items for enjoyment – music and books, treasures and mementoes.

Above If you plan storage as an integral part of your living room's design, you will discover a wide range of interesting possibilities. This high-level bookcase includes dramatic lighting.

Above left Even a small storage accessory can make a design statement. Keep a lookout for attractive magazine racks, storage boxes and CD racks.

Left and opposite For a truly tranquil space, devote one wall to custom-made storage and hide everything, from television to photo albums, behind floor-to-ceiling doors.

Above and below Rather than cram your shelves with objects, think of their arrangement as an art display. **Above right** It pays to think about the various sizes of your books before choosing shelves. In custom-made units, allow for low-level deep ones to hold coffee-table volumes, with lighter paperbacks higher up.

Built-in storage has the advantage of being tailor-made to suit your possessions, from book heights to television size, and can match your chosen decorative style. Try to think beyond the conventional option of a bookshelf and cupboard in each fireplace alcove, which makes a room look smaller. Shelves can be fitted around a door, just below the ceiling or spanning a bare wall. Closed storage options include a whole wall of panelling with individual doors that open to reveal cupboards; small alcoves inset into the wall, which hold everything from a television to a flower vase; or shallow cupboards, wall-mounted or built into an alcove, with frosted glass, MDF or Perspex doors.

The advantage of freestanding storage is that it comes with you when you move. Don't just think of bookshelves; other options include mix-and-match units offering shelves and cupboards, traditional commodes or storage ottomans, sideboards or even plan chests. Inside each piece of furniture, provide easy access to items like CDs and videos by placing them in cheap plastic racks, and keep bulky things such as photo albums low down so they are easy to lift out.

Plan where to house the technology at the outset, and the room will look slick. It is not an issue whether or not the television is on show, but do try to conceal trailing wires. The video player doesn't have to sit directly below the TV and is more practically stored in a cupboard next to the stereo, near the videos and CDs. If you must have a computer in the living room, screen it carefully from the main sitting area.

Opinions differ as to whether books should, or shouldn't, be included in a living room. In a very elegant room, many

Above In a partitioned living area, a 'window' with a shelf top is used to create an unexpected display area.
Left Long, shallow wall shelves provide the perfect opportunity for grouping family photos or artworks.
Below A sideboard can be a useful addition to a living room. This one doubles as a versatile storage option, with plenty of display space on top.

Right Particularly in tiny living rooms, it is essential that storage is decorative and multifunctional. This cabinet allows you to keep CDs and videos in order, while providing the base for an unusual daybed.
Below left If you don't have many shelves, pictures can be casually propped at floor level.
Below right Attractive storage boxes are the best way to counteract clutter. Keep the most frequently used items at the top of the pile.
Opposite Convert an unusual wall alcove – a redundant fireplace, for example – into dramatic storage.

colourful spines may detract from a deliberately rigid decorative scheme. In general, however, books add a lived-in, comfortable air. Spend some time arranging shelves neatly – otherwise, books quickly look messy.

The best living rooms bear the personality of their owner, so collect your favourite things there, be they serious artworks or stones gathered on the beach. Less is more in terms of display. A mantelpiece may need only a cluster of ceramic vases to look good. Instead of dotting paintings around the room, hang a cluster on a single wall, for an effect that is infinitely more arresting.

- Begin by **rationalizing** your requirements and ask yourself if particular items **really need to be stored** in a particular room.

- **Think laterally** about shelving – it can be positioned in alcoves, across a wall, **around a door** or just below the ceiling.

- However you store your stereo **or television**, make sure any trailing wires are concealed.

- Arrange shelves neatly, mixing **storage with display**. Several broad-fronted shelves look fabulous propped with framed family portraits.

- **Less is more** – stamp your personality on the room with displayed items, but avoid clutter.

living rooms

styles

Left While the contemporary look relies on boxy silhouettes and sharp corners, a living room that is genuinely relaxing needs some touches of softness too. A trendy fluffy rug or deep, welcoming upholstery can do a great deal to offset uncompromising modern lines.

Above Much new furniture is designed with a quirky twist, so look out for smaller items – from coffee tables to stools – that have a sense of humour.

Opposite Keep very modern rooms simple, but have fun repeating a chosen motif – a square, circle, triangle – in different ways. In this room, the square coffee tables and abstract canvases reinforce the cubic theme.

contemporary

Today's interior design has its roots in the uncompromising minimalism of the late 1990s. However, if you prefer a more comfortable take on the contemporary look, there are plenty of style elements you can adopt. And – who knows – the mantra of functionalism and order might just rub off a little.

Surfaces are vital to the contemporary style; if you get these right, the other details will fall into place. Surfaces should look expensive, even if they are not. Of course, you can spend a small fortune on solid-wood floors and polished-plaster walls. But you don't have to. There are plenty of good-looking equivalents, such as concrete or wood veneers laid over MDF, which cost half the price. And while you may need to invest in some new pieces of furniture, the sleek look, taken literally, needs only a few key pieces.

The ideal colour scheme is a variation on monochrome: white-on-white with natural tones or silvery metallics; or grey-on-grey, from graphite and gunmetal to pale blue-greys and off-whites. Soften these tones with accent colours, from lilac and scarlet to burnt orange, aubergine and citrus yellow, either in a piece of contemporary furniture, on walls or in cushions.

Above While hard surfaces are an important element of contemporary style, it is often advisable to save the concrete and marble for the kitchen. In the living room, add interest and colour with light-diffusing sandblasted glass, wooden floors or glossy spray-painted units.
Right Although it looks cool and elegant, an all-white room may seem clinical. Adding one piece of furniture in a rich tone – say, in a dark hardwood such as Macassar ebony or wenge – will warm it up considerably.

A rigorously designed modern interior requires a careful choice of furniture. The high street is full of good copies of designer pieces in the essential boxy and slim silhouettes. Armchairs are square-shaped, while a sofa may be long and low to the ground or L-shaped. Combine these pieces with glass- or stone-topped coffee tables and other furnishings in dark wood, brilliant gloss paint, lacquer or glass, all with stainless-steel detailing.

Fabrics need to be matt and slick, such as wools or leather, appropriate for the tight, figure-hugging outlines of sofas and chairs. Plains are most effective, but the occasional geometric or graphic print can look good.

Above left Loft apartments provide ideal backgrounds for the contemporary look, but a practised eye is needed to furnish their enormous, high-ceilinged rooms. Soften long lean outlines with smooth curves and squashy beanbags to balance the space.

Above and left Display is a vital part of the ultra-modern look, but keep it pared down. Use stark white walls for a gallery-like arrangement, and show off vases and accessories on shelves characterized by an almost sculptural minimalism.

smooth, sleek surfaces ...

Capture the textures of **gleaming glass**, smooth stone and the confident **gloss of lacquer**.

Select moody tones, from graphite to gunmetal, **biscuit to beige**.

Cutting-edge rooms demand **streamlined surfaces** and boxy furniture.

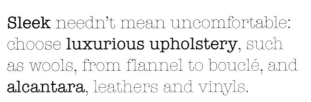

Sleek needn't mean uncomfortable: choose **luxurious upholstery**, such as wools, from flannel to bouclé, and **alcantara**, leathers and vinyls.

Store **cherished accessories** in built-in cupboards and choose one or two large-scale pieces for a **pared-down display**.

country

The country look has come of age in recent years. Gone are the frills, the shiny chintz and the china ornaments – superseded by rustic textiles, hard-working surfaces, and a faded colour palette, making the perfect backdrop for distinctive antique pieces, from furniture to textiles. It is unimportant if these items are distressed or worn; what counts is that they are unique, decorative and functional.

Left and far left For a traditional country feel, pick baggy loose covers rather than tight upholstery, and play with mismatched stripes and checks – a perennial country classic.

Above and top Combine contemporary furniture with natural materials, from stone and wood to homespun upholstery, for a modern take on rustic style.

As a decorative style, the country look is low-maintenance and family-friendly. Since it relies on a combination of all sorts of items, it can easily accommodate hand-me-down furniture, junk-shop buys and possessions collected over the years. You won't need to buy new pieces; just sort through what you already have. And rigorous sorting is crucial – country style does not imply jumble or clutter.

When deciding on your decor, whether for wall surfaces or furniture, remember that elements must look slightly battered or distressed; there is no place for brand-new upholstery or garish gilding. So conserve rather than restore. There is a definite charm to a 19th-century sofa with its stuffing peeking out or to mirrors whose glass is gently foxed. And if you don't have the real thing, you can always fake it. Many a new pine table or door can be given the country look with watered-down vinyl matt paint, some wire wool and finishing wax.

Above For a modern take on wall panelling and wooden floors, lighten them with white paint or pastel tones. Panelling styles can include tongue and groove or simple MDF squares.

Left If you are reupholstering your furniture, replace fussy frilled detailing with more graphic scallops or box pleats, or a soft Greek-style buttoned mattress.

On walls, you can achieve the worn-out rustic look with dead-matt emulsion paint in faded shades – or, for a genuinely earthy feel, strip off all the wallpaper and leave the patterns of the plaster underneath. Consider, too, the appeal of painted or unpainted brickwork. Wallpaper certainly harmonizes with the country look, but choose faded shades and avoid small or over-fussy patterns.

In terms of colour, the exact shade does not matter as much as the tone. Fresh pastels or any colours with too much white should be avoided in favour of washed-out or muddy tones. Instead of fresh white paintwork, choose one of the 'old' whites available from specialist paint ranges. Alternatively, experiment with woodwork in the same tone as the wall colour – always in eggshell, never gloss.

A tantalizing combination of textiles is a crucial part of country style. At the really traditional end, there are overblown faded chintzes, needlepoints, tapestries, patchworks and paisleys in classic patterns and textures. For a simpler look, choose ginghams, madras cottons and stripes, from ticking to deckchair canvas. Think about contrasting different textures, such as deep-pile velvet with tight-woven cottons. And mix your patterns with plenty of plain fabrics, which is the key to keeping the country look simple.

This page The focus of a country living room should be a welcoming sofa or daybed, piled high with cushions. The look is about mix and match, so contrast cushion sizes and shapes as well as patterns. Patchwork, the quintessential rustic textile, is trendy again, with many eye-catching versions available on the high street.

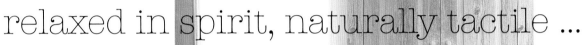

relaxed in spirit, naturally tactile ...

Nothing should seem new; your rooms should look as if they have evolved naturally.

Country style is cheap and its **classic looks endure**.

A **mixture of textiles** is a key part of the rustic look – team **faded chintz** with ticking, for example.

Country homes combine warmth, comfort and **a relaxed mood.**

fresh flowers, **candles and books** add to the ambience.

if you lack **inspiration,** nature's tones provide the perfect **earthy palette.**

cosy & informal

Top Low-slung and slim, retro furniture is perfect for a trendy, chilled-out living room. For a more up-to-date, sophisticated feel, stick to neutral upholstery.

Above It is fun (and still relatively cheap) to amass a collection of retro ceramics or lighting. Put it on display and let everyone enjoy it.

Right and far right So much of today's furniture has a retro feel that it is easy to combine it with the genuine article. Spice up plains with some abstract textiles or cushions; or, for maximum impact, place a design classic chair centre-stage and enjoy its fluid outline.

retro

It seems that we cannot get enough of the retro look. From 1950s spiky-legged furniture to 1970s floral fabrics, it looks good with today's modern shapes and spans an enticing colour spectrum, from hot brights to kooky pastels.

If you are trying to steer your way through the retro maze, it helps to combine pieces with a sense of fun. And use them sparingly: a single kitsch 1950s lamp is attention-grabbing, but too many battered items will make a room look like a 20th-century museum. It is possible to buy new copies of classic designs, or you can search out stores that specialize in retro furniture. However, much more fun – and less expensive – is to hunt down finds in junk shops.

Raid **car-boot sales and junk shops**, even your parents' home – the odds are that the coffee table you remember from childhood is a **design classic** now.

The retro style is not about period authenticity – have fun and **enjoy the witty spirit** in which many retro pieces were designed.

mid-century classics

Less is more: one retro chair and a lamp can be all you need to give **a funky new twist** to a living room.

Use **1950s and 1960s fabrics** as one-off cushion covers or stretched across a canvas for retro wall art.

pair with sleek modern lines

Below If you find it confusing to attempt to combine different historical styles, stick to simple, symmetrical arrangements as a useful starting point.

Right Experiment with a mix of contemporary textiles and traditional furniture shapes. If you don't want to go the whole way and cover a Chesterfield in a Pucci print, then arrange cushions in modern abstract patterns against a plainly upholstered period sofa. Alternatively, cover a trendy new chair in a classic chintz.

Opposite There is a pleasing surprise factor in placing period furniture in a modern interior. Here, the contrast of leather and floral sofas in a whitewashed loft space creates a fresh and contemporary twist.

old & new

The freedom to mix items from various historical periods and decorative categories is guaranteed to result in exciting and highly personal looks.

This style is all about contrast – a giant beanbag against Georgian wood panelling, a modern lounge-lizard sofa set beside vintage chintz curtains, or junk-shop finds displayed in a minimal, gallery-like space. Whatever your style, aim for a fun, experimental mood, but to avoid the Miss Havisham cliché keep a tight rein on clutter. Mixing old and new is all about constant change, so when you bring the next great discovery home, put something else away.

Always look out for new finds – the old & new style is **constantly evolving**.

Highlight the clash of antique and modern with quirky decorative touches.

Throw your possessions into **sharp relief** against a simple, gallery-like interior.

a quirky & personal mix ...

can't be bought off the peg

'Old' does not have to mean antique – instead, it may be **junk or second-hand**.

'New' need not be a costly designer acquisition; it can be a **high-street bargain**.

Chaotic and noisy it may be, but family living is also sociable and fun. For parents and kids alike, there is incalculable merit to a living room where everyone can gather *en famille* or invite friends over for a get-together.

Great seating is crucial. Children love fun, versatile seating, particularly low-level options that can be drawn up to a coffee table for afternoon tea or for television-watching. Consider beanbags or seating cubes, which can look very sophisticated in leather or felt. Whatever the furniture, think robust rather than precious. You can help kids to keep things tidy by filling your storage cupboards with smaller labelled boxes for toys. And keep plenty of space free on lower shelves for their books.

family-friendly

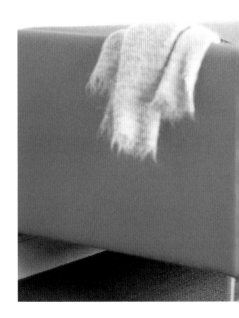

Opposite Kids love sprawling on the floor, so an unused fireplace is ideal for siting the television at a low level. Have fun with living-room furnishings, using splashes of bright colour, either as rugs, cushions or upholstery. **Left** Big sofas are great for sprawling on with friends. Choose a design that is long enough for gangly teenagers and upholstered in a cheerful, fuss-free fabric such as cotton or denim that's easily cleaned. **Above and below** When a living room doubles as a play space, there must be plenty of storage for quick tidy-ups. Here sturdy baskets, a retro sideboard and 1970s stacking compartments can all be stuffed with toys when playtime is over.

Bisect the space in L-shaped or **long narrow rooms** to create a main social area and **a quiet zone**.

Children like to be **near the floor**; carpets or rugs are soft on **little knees** (100 per cent wool is easy to clean).

room to play & relax ...

for all the family

Retouch painted walls to conceal sticky fingerprints; **patterned or textured** finishes hide marks

Children appreciate low-level seating and the **novelty** of **quirky furniture**.

Ask your children what **precious things** they would like to include in the decor.

cooking & eating spaces

elements

Left The designer has chosen an intriguing place to position this room divider, which incorporates sink, dishwasher and storage. It straddles a change of levels between rooms linked by a small flight of steps. The long unit encloses the kitchen work area to the left and separates it from the small, lower-level dining area.

Below Open-plan kitchen and living areas give a greater feeling of space, but sometimes you want to be shielded from the sights, sounds and smells of the kitchen. These sliding panels, suspended from the ceiling, offer a wonderful compromise.

planning the space

If you are designing a new kitchen or remodelling an old one, start by deciding what type of room would best suit your home and lifestyle. Will it be a family kitchen? Can it be opened up to the living room? Should it be separate from the dining area? Does it need to double as a laundry or home office? And is your kitchen's current location the best place for it – could it be moved to make better use of space, or might it be better accommodated in a new extension?

Left The island and wall units of this chic kitchen have been given a white finish that harmonizes with the wall colour, ensuring that the work area takes on a subsidiary role in the room. Only the vast hanging rack offers a visual contrast here.

Below A plan of the kitchen pictured on the left shows how the design has minimized the impact of the cooking zone and placed emphasis on the dining area and the window. When you enter this room, your attention is seized by the glass-topped table that stands in front of a large window overlooking the garden; meanwhile, the fixtures take second place, sitting neatly along the back wall. A couple of large fridge-freezers have been accommodated in the corner of the room.

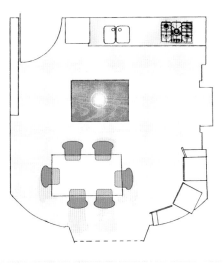

Consider how much and what style of cooking you do. How often do you shop? How often do you invite friends round? Do you prefer big parties or small intimate dinners? All these things have an impact on an ideal kitchen design. If you can cook in the way you like with minimal equipment and storage space, don't be tempted to line the room with unnecessary and expensive units. If you shop at the supermarket only once a month, you are likely to need a generous fridge as well as a separate freezer and extra cupboards.

Substantial changes to the layout of the room will affect plumbing and electrical wiring, so take these into account at an early stage. This is also the time to consider whether the lighting scheme needs upgrading and to decide if you need

Opposite, above A horseshoe layout allows a division between the kitchen and the dining or living area while letting the cook observe children or talk to guests.
Opposite, below This kitchen includes a breakfast bar for quick meals as well as a table for more formal dining.
This page Whether you opt for a wall of fitted cupboards or a more conventional below-and-above countertop arrangement, plenty of storage space means that you can keep your kitchen worktops clear.

new appliances, such as a small cooker, a big professional-style range or a dishwasher.

Successful kitchen design reveals itself in your ease of movement in the 'work triangle' between cooker, fridge and sink. Avoid siting fridge doors where they would crash into oven doors, and don't place a table in the middle of the busy area between these three elements. Build in plenty of countertop space beside the main fixtures and appliances, so there is room to put down food, hot pans and plates, as well as for chopping and other preparation of ingredients.

- Major reorganization is likely to involve the plumbing, **electrical or gas** services.

- **Lighting upgrades** should be carried out before other works begin.

- Site appliances for **comfort and convenience** – sketch alternative layouts for the cooker, fridge and sink triangle.

storage

This page Open or glass-fronted shelves can retain a minimal look, provided you keep them tidy and ordered. Whether the shelves form part of a sleek bespoke wooden unit or a professional-style stainless-steel kitchen, the effect is urban and contemporary.

Opposite The owners of this much-used kitchen take pleasure in showing off their beautiful pots, shiny accessories and utensils.

There is a universal law about storage: no matter how much you have, you will always need more. So, if you are lucky enough to have room for manoeuvre, be generous in your estimates. When it comes to deciding on the type of storage you want, most people divide into two camps: those who like to celebrate their possessions by putting them on show and those who prefer everything hidden tidily out of sight. Knowing which group you belong to will help you to choose storage appropriate to your needs.

fitted & unfitted

Fitted kitchens with their runs of wall and floor units usually offer plenty of storage space, but it is worth comparing this capacity with other types of storage such as an old-fashioned dresser. This single piece of furniture can hold an enormous amount of kitchenware and has the advantage of combining closed-in cupboards and open display shelving. If you like open shelving, install a couple of cupboards to hold unattractive items such as cleaning materials and buckets. If you prefer cupboards, try to include at least some open shelving – if only to provide visual relief from the oppression of closed doors.

There are two types of fitted kitchen cupboards: the mass-produced, cheap and cheerful variety sold in flat packs; and the upmarket kind that can be tailor-made to your individual design and in the materials of your choice. Although it is unlikely that factory-produced units will be made of the finest woods or built with exquisite

cabinet-making skills, the best of them do an amazing job. They incorporate many useful features, are available in an extensive range of shapes and sizes, and can be individualized by the simple addition of doors and handles of your own choice. On the other hand, if you can afford a taste of genuine luxury, why not hire talented kitchen designers and cabinet-makers to produce works of exceptional beauty and longevity?

Above left Among the excellent features incorporated in these sheer-fronted units is a vertical sliding-drawer larder.
Above right Back-lit cupboards and shelving not only make it easy to find items but also constitute an intriguing feature – almost like an artwork – in the kitchen.
Left Display your crockery to make it quick and easy to find the right plates and cups. Or mix glass- and solid-fronted units for an interesting chequerboard pattern.
Opposite Elements of the unfitted style of storage are often borrowed from the professional realm. An efficient restaurant kitchen will almost certainly include objects such as hanging racks for a whole range of utensils, catering-size metal baking trays and stainless-steel trolleys.

People who enjoy the shapes, colours, textures and simple beauty of kitchen accoutrements can find unfitted storage irresistibly appealing. While the unfitted kitchen exerts a powerful aesthetic appeal, and provides the additional attractions of comfort and informality, it can also be surprisingly practical. Indeed, the contemporary unfitted look is ideal for anyone who moves house frequently because it makes it easy to take some of your favourite objects to your new home.

The unfitted kitchen is also appropriate for anyone on a limited budget since, compared with a fitted style, it can be moderately inexpensive to design and put together, and it allows the flexibility to build on when you find another piece of furniture that fits.

details & ergonomics

The huge range of utensils, pans and accessories now on offer means that the modern cook is spoiled for choice, and the design of kitchen storage has necessarily been elevated to an exercise in space engineering. However, attention to detail can make your kitchen a much more satisfying place in which to live and work, and when your kitchen design is complete you will know that the job has been well done.

When planning storage, begin by identifying the type of material to be stored. Think about how you shop and how you cook. Aim to ensure that often used items are close to you. Think of yourself as the hub of a series of concentric circles. As they radiate out from the centre, they represent storage areas for items in different degrees of use. The less something is used, the farther away (or higher up) it can be stored.

The area between your waist and shoulder height when you are standing is the best place for storing most items in frequent use – it is readily accessible and means that you don't have to stretch or bend down too often. Lightweight items should be stored at the top of units, while heavier items are best placed lower down.

Above Among the many ingenious devices specially designed for small spaces is this liftable panel which opens to reveal a toaster.

Right In this well-organized kitchen, the stove is flanked by triple-layer cooking-pot stands, which are themselves flanked by drawer units. The stands are handsome items in themselves, comprising slices of dark grey Delabole slate within a stainless-steel frame.

Far right A brilliant piece of design, this chopping board and trolley can be wheeled around the kitchen to wherever it is needed. When not in use, it can simply be stowed away in the cupboard.

- **Make a list** of the types of item you need to store.

- Decide if you prefer things on display or **out of sight**.

- Consider where to locate the items you **use most often** (baking or pasta-making equipment, for example).

- **Auctions and second-hand shops** can be good sources for storage bargains.

- An **all-in-one unit** is ideal if you don't cook much or have little space.

- **Commission a tailor-made kitchen** only if you have a big budget and are planning to stay in your home for a long time.

- **Don't overlook details** – build in time to research finishing touches.

Above Even in the hardest-working kitchens there Is room for a bit of fun. This owner clearly has a sense of humour and has subverted the restrained stainless-steel look with a decorative storage rack filled with items in beautiful and colourful packaging.

Far left An unusual but effective approach to unfitted storage is to make a frame or shelves into which baskets can be slotted.

Left Kitchen designers are forever coming up with space-saving ideas. A door-fitted rack is an example of how to make the most of difficult corner space.

surfaces

Designed to withstand the endless wear and tear associated with chopping and preparing food, as well as water splashes, worktops and splashbacks are also expected to scrub up beautifully when the cooking is over. In addition, kitchen surfaces provide an excellent visual and textural opportunity to draw together other stylistic elements of the room's design.

Wood is a perennial favourite for worktops. Pale maple or beech can be found in countless kitchens, but darker and more exotically patterned woods are making an appearance. If you want to incorporate a wooden surface, you need to decide how it will be finished. For example, a beech chopping-board area should be left completely untreated. This tough wood withstands a huge amount of chopping, can cope with fairly hot pans, and scrubs up very well after use.

If you prefer your wood counter to look pristine, a surface finishing is required. Products including Danish oil and tung oil soak into the wood fibres and set hard to repel water and oil splashes, but they need regular maintenance. A tough varnish finish requires minimal maintenance but cannot be used unprotected for chopping up food or putting down hot pans.

Stainless-steel worktops and splashbacks look stunning and, if they are of a high enough grade, will last a lifetime.

As you use it and clean it, the surface will become covered in a mesh of scratches and marks that develops into a mellow burnish, making stainless steel one of the few worktop materials that improves with age and wear.

Another smooth, durable material that can be welded into long runs and formed into shapes for sinks is a manmade product called Corian. A composite of natural minerals and acrylic resin, it is heat-resistant, stain-resistant and available in numerous colours. Likewise, plastic laminate surfaces are produced in hundreds of colours and patterns, sold by the mile in DIY stores. They are tough, easy to clean and come at a fraction of the cost of most other surfaces.

Natural stone and slate worktops have become increasingly sought after in recent years. An enormous slice of shaped marble is a beautiful sight to behold and adds an air of luxury to an elegant kitchen. It is also very expensive, especially when it includes a hole for a recessed sink and perhaps also tapered grooves for a draining board.

Other stone-type options include stone composites. Several companies are now producing interesting materials by mixing lumps of marble or small speckles of quartzite into a bonding agent such as a resin or a concrete. These are moderately expensive, but do look striking. A further stone-style option is concrete. Forget old-fashioned notions of grey and boring – concrete now comes in all sorts of colours and textures, and can be delivered as a ready-cast worktop or made for you on site.

All types of stone have a porous surface, so ask your supplier what sort of treatment is recommended to avoid staining.

- **Wood** is an excellent material for work surfaces; for a perfect finish, seal it with varnish or Danish oil.

- **Stainless steel** is heatproof and virtually indestructible; a professional grade lasts a lifetime and improves with age and use.

- **Corian** is an acrylic and mineral product that can be joined and formed as needed.

- **Laminate** is tough, good value and sold in an enormous range of colours and patterns.

- **Stone and slate** are beautiful, expensive, luxurious - and found in endless variety.

- **Concrete** can be cast specifically to suit your needs, then polished, finished and sealed.

- **Splashbacks** come in a variety of materials such as stone, stainless steel, glass and Perspex.

Flooring is a major component in any design scheme, setting the tone for the whole room. In a kitchen it can also devour a large part of your budget, so take care to research well and choose wisely. A canny option is to combine different flooring materials – keep warm-toned luxurious timber for the dining area and lay durable stone, slate or linoleum in the cooking area.

Left Small black and white ceramic tiles produce a stunning geometric pattern which looks particularly handsome alongside the black units, white ceramic Belfast sink and stainless-steel detailing.
Below For a sheer and shimmering mirror finish, specialist high-gloss floor paint has been used on this old wood parquet.
Opposite Bare floorboards wear well and have a pleasing rustic feel.

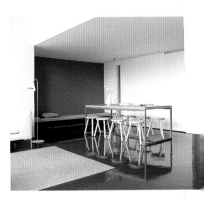

flooring

Natural materials such as timber, stone and brick look at home in just about any kitchen. They are hardwearing and durable, but they need protection to keep them looking their best. Timber flooring is available in finishes ranging from untreated, solid planks to factory-made laminates with a protective vinyl coating. It is important to protect solid, unfinished boards with a varnish, oil or wax polish. Cork tiles also benefit from a protective coating. Some tiles are sold with a transparent vinyl finish, but if you have chosen a natural tile it can be sealed with a regular floor varnish.

Other natural materials include hundreds of intriguing stones, marbles and slates, as well as manmade composites that combine quartz with a resin or cement bonding. Although stone is very hard, it is also porous, so ask your supplier for advice on the most appropriate sealant.

The fashion for wood and stone floors has left sheet and tile finishes in the shade, but there is a huge amount to be said for vinyl, linoleum and rubber. They are warm, soft, lightweight, relatively easy to lay, fairly forgiving of slightly uneven floors – and the choice is more extensive than ever. On top of that, they look good in just about any style of kitchen, they are considerably cheaper than wood or stone alternatives, require no finishing and are very easy to keep clean. Also available are big panels of stainless steel or aluminium, which are unusual and eyecatching, and look great held in place with lines of neat rivets, but are slippery to walk on when wet.

Below, from left to right Speckled patterns, such as this composite made from coloured stones, are highly practical in heavily used family kitchens – they don't require constant cleaning. Diamond and square tiles create a lively pattern. Sterlingboard tiles are an inexpensive option and produce an interesting effect. Studded rubber is stylish, modern and hard-wearing.

- The **floor base** should be sound and stable, and strong enough to carry the weight of your chosen material.

- **Timber** is a sympathetic option, ranging from ready-made interlocking systems to solid boards.

- Hardwearing **cork** is much underrated; it is an efficient sound-absorber, a good looker, and feels warm to the touch.

- **Stone** is a big investment but provides a tough finish that will last a lifetime.

- **Concrete** – painted, waxed or varnished – has become a favourite in modern interiors.

- Stylish and excellent value, **linoleum and vinyl** are the unsung heroes of the kitchen.

Above Sheet-metal flooring is a stylish, hard-working option for a kitchen, with a strong industrial aesthetic, but it can be slippery. **Right** Timber flooring introduces a sense of warmth and texture to an all-white room that is otherwise sleek and hard-edged. A solid, machine-made flooring such as cut stone slabs could have made this room feel chilly and uninviting.

lighting

Kitchen lighting must give good, safe illumination for work areas and comfortable ambient lighting for the main part of the room, and be flexible enough to cope with a variety of dining situations. To achieve the range of effects you desire, you will probably need to incorporate a selection of different lighting types.

Above Lighting should be attractive as well as practical. In this room shelf-fixed downlighters illuminate the work surface and the wall-fixed lamp on an extending arm can be directed to where light is needed.

Right The choice of lighting types for kitchens is vast: from suspended pendant lights with brushed-aluminium or glass shades to these unusual office-style lamps on articulated arms and tiny, sparkling fittings which can be built into the underside of units. The best lighting schemes will incorporate a number of different styles to achieve results that are both practical and aesthetic.

When you start to plan a scheme, take stock of the lighting that is already in existence. Make notes about where it falls short, which lights need to be moved or added, and what style of lighting you would like to install. This is also the moment to have your wiring checked and to decide whether it would be helpful to have more electrical sockets.

The importance of good functional lighting, or task lighting, cannot be overestimated. A kitchen is full of potential hazards – sharp knives, hot water and heavy pans, to name but a few – and it is the site of more accidents than any other room in the home. Task lighting should provide worktops with high levels of illumination and be positioned to ensure that you are not standing in your own shadow. It is a good idea to install these functional lights on a separate circuit from the main room lights, so that they can be dimmed or turned off altogether when they are not needed.

In addition to task lighting, the room will require a general wash of ambient illumination that helps to shape the overall space. This is usually provided by a central pendant light, wall lights or a ceiling-fixed track that can be angled to direct light across the ceiling or down the walls. Sparkling-white

halogen lights have become a popular choice for use in track systems or to highlight particular features of a room.

Fluorescent tubes, attached just beneath wall cupboards, are most frequently used for worktop lighting. An attractive alternative to the fluorescent tube is the tungsten tube, which emits a lovely, soft, creamy-coloured light. Then there is the trusty tungsten lightbulb – useful in pendant lights suspended over tables and for large spotlights.

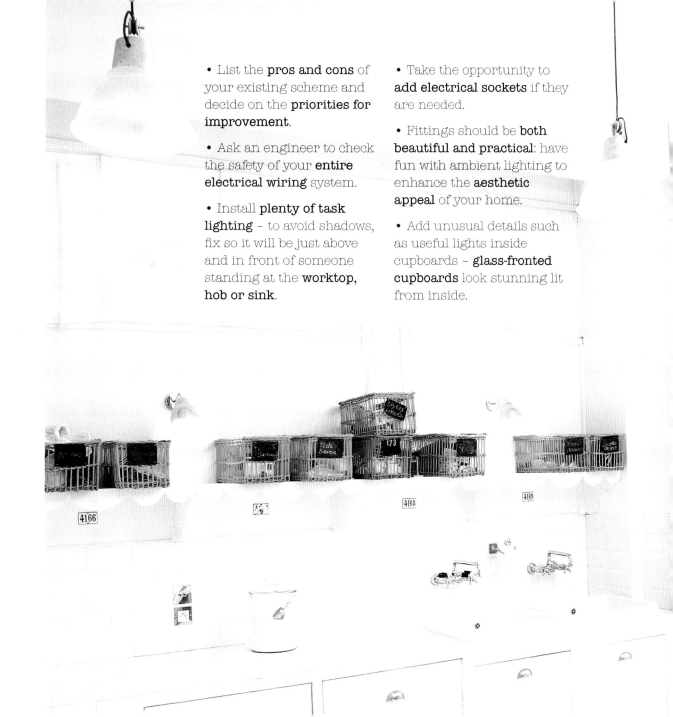

- List the **pros and cons** of your existing scheme and decide on the **priorities for improvement**.

- Ask an engineer to check the safety of your **entire electrical wiring** system.

- Install **plenty of task lighting** – to avoid shadows, fix so it will be just above and in front of someone standing at the **worktop, hob or sink**.

- Take the opportunity to **add electrical sockets** if they are needed.

- Fittings should be **both beautiful and practical**: have fun with ambient lighting to enhance the **aesthetic appeal** of your home.

- Add unusual details such as useful lights inside cupboards – **glass-fronted cupboards** look stunning lit from inside.

fixtures & appliances

It is easy to be attracted by minimal designs and sophisticated models that promise to run the kitchen for you. Before you buy, think carefully about what you cook and how you cook it, and base your selection of fixtures and appliances on what seems most appropriate to your needs.

Above Incorporating a worktop, a double-ringed hob and an inset circular sink and tap, this sweep of stainless steel makes impressively good use of a confined space.
Left This capacious fridge and freezer unit is ideal for a large family kitchen where lots of foods need to be stored in a cool place. The doors are finished in the same sleek metal as the rest of the kitchen, which helps to reduce the visual bulk of the appliance.

sinks & taps

The wet area of the kitchen demands as much design thought as elsewhere. You will probably use the sink every time you prepare food, so your choice should be based on practical requirements. If you have ever had to wash roasting trays in a tiny circular sink, you will know how frustrating it can be.

For something simple and exceptionally good value, a standard pressed-steel sink unit is hard to beat. Among the other delights on offer are sinks of every shape in beaten copper, glass, enamel, acrylic, and the handsome and trusty Belfast sink in white ceramic. In recent years there has been a move away from in-built draining boards. Be warned: a sink without a draining board may look wonderfully sleek and

minimal, but once those roasting trays have been washed, you will want to leave them to drain before stowing them away.

There is a huge variety of taps available, from old-fashioned crosshead sets to modern mixers with a multitude of additional features. Since taps are probably the most frequently used fitting in a kitchen, it is worth investing in the best possible quality.

Left and below left Large sinks and draining areas take up space but are welcome in kitchens that must accommodate styles of cooking that use large trays or awkwardly shaped items such as woks.
Above right In this reinvention of the Belfast sink, a timber 'chest' sink sits inside a specially made curved concrete cradle.
Right Two sinks are always better than one – this arrangement leaves one for washing, one for rinsing.

- The sink's **size and shape** should reflect your style of cooking – **if you regularly cook roasts**, for example, it must be large enough to take a roasting tray.

- **Draining boards** are more useful than you might think: if space is restricted, a small draining area is **better than none at all**.

- Taps can **incorporate** a multitude of added features, but think hard about whether you really need **the extras**.

- **Water softeners** installed in hard-water areas prevent the build-up of limescale deposits and **consequent damage** to stainless-steel sinks and taps.

Above Good-quality crosshead taps are a wise investment, but don't take things too seriously – cheer the place up with varnished 1950s postcards.

Left Taps are becoming increasingly multifunctional. It is still possible to buy reliable old-fashioned sets with crosshead tops, but modern designs offer pull-out ends and flexible spouts for hosing down salads.

fridges & freezers

Long regarded as boring white boxes, fridge-freezers have at last gained recognition as great design objects, and models are appearing in a range of shapes, sizes and colours to suit people's tastes and their shopping habits.

An integrated fridge is an expensive luxury, but it does have the advantage that it sits behind a cupboard door without taking up a vast amount of space. Other options include choosing big boxy fridges and then having a frame made to disguise its bulk. Among the most attractive innovations are fridges with glass fronts, which mimic those in professional kitchens and shops. These are sleek pieces of design, often made with glass set inside a stainless-steel frame.

Most of us are happy to make do with a half or third of the fridge devoted to shelves or pull-out trays for frozen goods. If you need more capacity, there are upright or chest freezers in a whole range of sizes, but these have unfortunately remained untouched by developments in contemporary design.

Above Refrigerators need not be concealed behind cupboard doors. If you have chosen a stunning fridge, it will stand happily on show and look great. The old American-style refrigerator – whose characterful, rounded shape made it much sought after in its day – is enjoying a popular revival. Likewise, modern brightly coloured models are particularly attractive.

Left As the fridge has taken over from the pantry, many families are opting for the capacious American-style double refrigerator, or buying a pair of fridges or a fridge and freezer, to stand side by side.

Right State-of-the-art hobs are dramatically increasing the responsiveness of electrical appliances.

Centre right Tiny electrical hobs are ideal for tasks such as making espresso coffee or warming soup. They are very efficient and wonderful space-savers in a small kitchen – ideal for anyone who does little cooking.

Far right The old-fashioned range is more than just a cooker: it is the hub of the kitchen where people love to warm themselves against the toasty hot doors. The range can also double as a boiler to supply the home with hot water and central heating.

Below A vast stainless-steel hob with different types of gas burners and two close-down covers is the main feature of this exciting set-up.

Opposite, main picture If you dislike having appliances on show, stow away the microwave when it is not in use.

ovens & hobs

When it comes to identifying the ideal cooking set-up, most people fall into one of two categories: those who like a built-in oven with a separate hob and those who prefer a freestanding cooker. As a rule, the built-in oven appeals most to those who like order, fingertip control and the latest technology. Freestanding cookers have a more diverse fan club.

There are two main types of freestanding cooker. At one end of the spectrum is the regular slide-in machine with an eye-level grill. At the other is the great big, semi-professional cooker or country range. The principal differences between the two concern size and price. While the humble machine is comparable in price to a weekend break, the range will cost the equivalent of a small car.

- **Freestanding or built-in?** Start by identifying your preferred style of oven.

- **Country or professional?** If you choose to have a freestanding model, decide which style is best suited to the design and layout of your room.

- **Gas or electric?** Many cooks feel the best combination is a gas hob and an electric oven. The fuel available in your area will have an important bearing on your choice.

- **State-of-the-art or straightforward?** If you can't understand the controls in the showroom, it will mean hours poring over the manual.

Making the decision to install a built-in cooker and hob in separate locations will give you much more flexibility in the layout of your kitchen. The oven can be located almost anywhere under the countertop or at waist level in a wall-fixed unit. Hobs can then be positioned in one of any number of places on the countertop.

Base your final choice of oven and hob on your style of cooking. If you are an infrequent cook, are you prepared to spend a small fortune on equipment that will remain largely unused? If you are a regular cook, do you have the budget to invest in the cooker of your dreams?

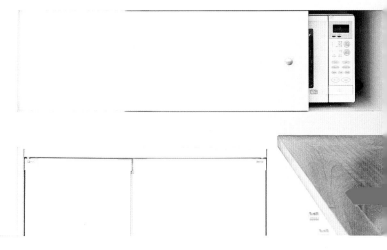

cooking & eating spaces

styles

contemporary

Ultra-modern kitchens are essays in exquisite finishes and expert craftsmanship. They are rigorously designed and highly industrialized products with controlled, crisp edges, which seem absolutely appropriate in big, stripped-back, minimally furnished apartments, converted warehouses and former factory buildings. However, while such a style of kitchen is frequently associated with loft apartments, it can look just as good in an old barn or farmhouse.

Far left The loft apartment is the natural home for a contemporary-style kitchen. The factory-made stainless-steel units complement the tough, urban warehouse aesthetic with its metal windows and smooth plastered walls.

Left and below This stainless-steel design is based on the professional kitchens found in restaurants and hotels, but luxuries such as a marble splashback would never be found in a commercial kitchen.

Among the most distinctive features of the contemporary kitchen style are runs of built-in floor and wall cupboards. Such cupboards might be painted or lacquered, or designed to incorporate a metal-mesh or glass-panelled front. Work surfaces in such kitchens are commonly made of stone, concrete, metal or a tough and durable manmade material such as Corian or a quartz composite.

Appliances are ultra-modern and probably built in. Lighting features low-voltage and mains halogen lamps to provide a sparkling white light. Where there is room for a dining table, it is almost certain to be contemporary in style, too.

There is plenty of room for experimentation. People who want a more professional-looking finish will opt for durable and crisp hard surfaces: stainless steel for units, worktops and appliance doors; stone for flooring; glass for door fronts or shelves; and white or neutral-coloured walls. These elements will be complemented by plain and elegant accessories, such

Above True to the modern look, every feature and surface in this kitchen has been carefully thought out and beautifully finished. The mid-tone wood appears in the monumental room-divider unit and on the smaller wall units opposite. The palette is completed with the use of opaque glass on cupboard fronts and a shiny black table top.
Left The sleek finishes and state-of-the-art oven leave no doubt that this is the kitchen of someone who appreciates high-quality modern design. The table and bench, in a darker wood than the units, share the same aesthetic.

Left In this exquisite example of fine engineering, stainless-steel doors are topped by a continuous stainless-steel work surface and built-in sink. Slender open shelves show off white crockery, stainless steel and glassware.

Right Wood is used in a restrained and modern way in these mesh-fronted cupboards.

Below right Designed half a century ago by Arne Jacobsen, these Series 7 chairs still look new, and help to create an interior that is both contemporary and timeless.

Bottom right The warm walnut tones of these kitchen cupboards offset the coolness of stainless steel, white laminate and Perspex.

as contemporary-style chrome taps, industrial-style electrical sockets and light switches, professional pans and utensils, and simple white crockery.

Mixing metal and wood is another way to interpret the contemporary style. The ideal setting for a 'mixed' kitchen is a space that is well illuminated by natural sunlight and which has beautifully finished floors and plain painted or tiled walls. The industrial toughness of metal can be offset by timber finishes. Stainless steel and chrome look great with a whole range of wood tones, from honey-coloured beech and maple to the richest, darkest wenge. Open-grained softwoods such as pine do not combine well with metal, but stainless steel does have a strong affinity with plywood. The key to success in this style is to restrict the combination of metal and wood to just two different materials, and certainly no more than three. Try stainless-steel worktops with metal-and-beech cupboard doors and then beech again for the floor, for example. Explore the upmarket contemporary-style kitchen showrooms to see how this works best. Finishing touches are crucial, too: beautiful joinery, long metal handles or push-release mechanisms for doors, and lighting that makes the place sparkle.

Modular units – in painted, lacquered, tough laminate or sheet-steel finishes – are the **building blocks** of the style.

Order and organization are key, with **closed storage space** and surfaces kept clear of equipment and accessories.

streamlined modern elements ...

Lighting features crisp halogen lamps, but **build in softer options** such as aluminium or glass pendants.

Furniture has metal frames; tables are **topped with glass, laminate, stone** or highly polished wood.

Invest in **high-quality fixtures** and workmanship.

from the professional kitchen

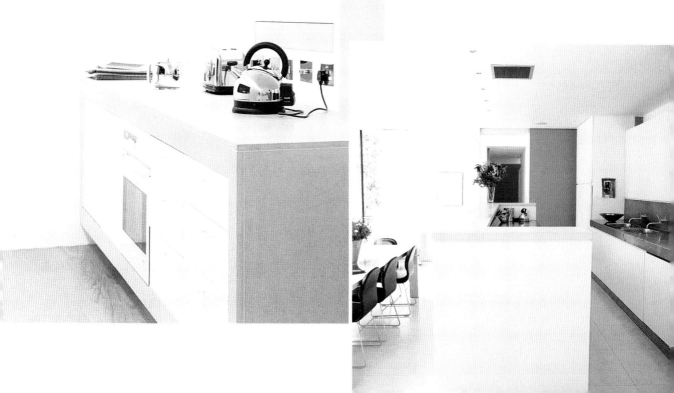

country

The country style has its roots in the traditional farmhouse kitchen – which could be found virtually anywhere in the Western world. Ideas and details are drawn from places as far apart as Tuscany and Devon, Philadelphia and Provence. While the country kitchen is a nest of nostalgia, it remains a highly functional workplace that has stood the test of time. Hefty cast-iron stoves and ranges are ideal for family cooking; dressers have great storage capacity; highly durable floors can withstand most of what is thrown at them; and farmhouse tables are rugged and virtually indestructible.

Left The generous proportions of this room and the use of wood for cupboards and flooring combine to make this a robust workplace. From the rack of pans to the pots of utensils and the big stove, this is a place for serious cooking. Hanging baskets of vegetables and fruit add a nice finishing touch.

Right The country look is exemplified by the big Belfast sink, the racks of pots hung to dry, the wood-finished walls, and herbs growing on the sunny window ledge.

Below, left and right There is a jolly chaos to the country look, a sense of abundance and generosity. In contrast to its urban cousin, the country kitchen is a place for pattern. Whether your style is cottage rosebuds or retro prints, fabrics are indispensable in completing the look.

Although today's country kitchen bears a strong resemblance to its predecessors, under the scrubbed-down surfaces lurk the dishwashers, fridge-freezers and lighting systems of modern life. After establishing the traditional character of the space by installing an enamel stove or range, some form of natural flooring and appropriate furniture, it becomes possible gradually to mix in a few modern items – perhaps a run of fitted cupboards or a track of spotlights.

The skill in creating a successful mixture of old and new is to ensure that the interventions are sensitive to the overall look. Anything that is too highly finished will jar with the mellowness of the room. The same thinking should be applied to details such as tiling and taps, shelving and furniture – items should all maintain an air of simplicity.

A visit to an architectural salvage yard could yield some real finds in the shape of period sinks, tiles or furniture. Take care when purchasing second-hand goods – some older items

Above This room epitomizes rural style. The chequered fabric of the sofa takes front of stage, while the small kitchen behind it features lots of open shelves for showing off intriguing objects. The wooden floor completes the look.

Right From the display of white enamel saucepans on top of the plate rack to the built-in dresser with its blue and white china, this restrained country look has been carefully orchestrated. The room has a limited palette of white and wood, with interest added in the blue of the china, the wicker basket and the garlic hanging by the stove.

Left In this example of retro rural style, the blue and white theme conveys a strong 1950s feel, and the painted cupboard combines simplicity with practicality.
Far left A white theme with accents of red is a real breath of fresh air. This is clearly a rural kitchen, but it has an interesting modern edge.
Below The Shaker style of kitchen works equally well in the town and the country. The elegantly designed cupboards are the colour of clotted cream – a soft effect enhanced by the arch detail on the doors.

such as taps might no longer be compatible with modern plumbing. There are also plenty of shops selling new kitchen products in retro styles: enamelled freestanding fridges, 1950s-style food mixers, Formica-topped tables and chairs, and a vast array of period lamps.

Among the most popular versions of the country style in recent years have been the Shaker kitchens imported from the USA and kitchens with a lighter, Scandinavian look. In both cases, many classic elements survive: natural flooring materials, wood-built units and countertops, and ceramic Belfast sinks. Yet today's version is more sophisticated, more efficient even, than the original.

The country-style kitchen can work just as well in an urban setting as it does in a more rural context. Its look are less important than its general ambience, which is comfortable, welcoming and informal.

easy-to-live-with style ...

You need not spend a fortune to achieve this **homely, welcoming** look.

Flagstones, large terracotta tiles or wooden **floorboards** set the scene.

Worktops are in **pale beech or maple**, or for a sophisticated alternative choose **slate or marble**.

Research your **period look** – visit museums, read books – and keep your eyes open for the furnishings and all-important **details that reflect the style**.

Build up a collection of **antique kitchen utensils**, such as **butter moulds**, milk jugs, stone hot-water bottles.

using natural materials

compact

Although there is no room for waste or error when planning the layout of a small kitchen, there is plenty of opportunity for big ideas to make even the tiniest area satisfy your needs. A small galley might initially look like the toughest of design challenges, but in many ways the smaller the kitchen the easier the job. There are many examples to follow: minuscule kitchens in barges and boats, all-in-one studio kitchens, and the cupboard-sized operations found in many offices.

Left This horseshoe-shaped layout, with cooker at one end, makes an efficient cooking space for one person, with practically all you need within arm's reach.

Below Fitted cupboards ensure that no space is wasted and make it possible to stow everything away, including cookery books. With clutter out of sight, the kitchen is kept in an orderly fashion.

Opposite In addition to providing storage space, the custom-made wall cupboards disguise an extractor vent. Fitted to the underside of the cupboards is the base of the extractor; the action of drawing this forward switches on the fan and built-in lights. The rest of the unit is housed inside the cupboards.

Left Small kitchens often represent a triumph of space engineering. This one combines the basics of sink, hob, microwave and fridge, and features an unusual tier of cupboards at ceiling level for items least often in use.

Below A good idea in small kitchens is to have open shelves above the work surface. In a confined space – particularly a narrow galley – shelves tend to be less oppressive than a row of closed cupboards.

Be optimistic. Small can be beautiful. With a little invention it is possible to create delicious, full-scale meals using no more than a double electric hob. The first step is to take a look at the space available and make realistic plans. Devote as much time as possible to planning your layout – time spent working on paper will save frustrations later on. What sort of cooking do you want to carry out? What style of kitchen do you prefer? The sleek contemporary look is probably the most space-efficient, but there is nothing to prevent you creating a friendly, country-style space.

Left This cupboard kitchen has all you need for even quite complex cooking. The detailing is exquisite, with sheer, easy-to-clean surfaces, plenty of storage and a convenient hanging rail for utensils. When the cooking and clearing up is done, simply pull the doors closed.
Below Even when space is very limited, try to keep windows free from obstructions. Good lighting can prevent the smallest kitchens from feeling cramped.

Start with the basics: a sink, refrigerator, hob and oven. Scaled-down versions of each of these are now on the market. It is even possible to find countertop dishwashers and washing machines.

With the appliances in mind, assess how much storage you require. The key to a successful compact kitchen is to use every available nook. The cleverest kitchens incorporate all sorts of great ideas, including large drawers at floor level in place of kick boards, swing-out corner carousels, cupboards that stretch to the ceiling, fold-down tables, and so on. Consider also whether a cupboard can be located elsewhere in the home. For example, a dresser in the dining room could house crockery and cutlery, freeing up a kitchen cupboard to accommodate the washing machine.

Try to maximize the natural light available in the room, and make sure you have artificial lighting that is genuinely efficient. A compact kitchen can indeed be a challenge, but when designed with care it can also be a real pleasure to cook in.

reduced to bare essentials ...

Be realistic in your aims and **resist crowding the space** – dispense with items that you rarely use.

Opt for **scaled-down** appliances and use every **nook and cranny**.

Imitate **innovative design ideas**, such as big drawers at floor level instead of kick boards.

Sheer, shining surfaces in pale colours reflect light, giving **a sense of space**.

Built-in cupboards provide **maximum storage** space.

Relocate items, such as the washing machine, to **elsewhere in the home**.

Keep **windows unobstructed** and ensure there are high levels of artificial lighting.

small spaces succeed

family-friendly

As the hub of the home, the kitchen is a place for family and friends to congregate. The style should be relaxed, flexible and welcoming as well as safe, hygienic and highly durable. Don't be afraid to introduce a few splashes of colour and interesting details such as blackboards, toy cupboards and a play corner. An open-plan design is perfect for families, enabling adults to do the cooking while keeping a watchful eye on children while they play, eat or complete their homework.

Far left Two large fridge-freezers are sited in the corner of this kitchen behind blackboard-covered doors. Parents can use the upper part of the blackboards for writing messages, while children use the lower portion.

Left Open-plan living can be ideal for familes with young children, making it possible for parents to prepare meals in the kitchen area while keeping an eye on the children. This home has a small family dining area close to the kitchen, as well as a larger dining area for more formal entertaining.

Below Irresistible child-friendly details such as these chair backs make mealtimes more enjoyable.

The key to a successful family-friendly kitchen is to create a space where children and adults can spend time together and separately, both doing what they want to do without getting under each other's feet. Having adequate space to accommodate everyone is vital, so very small kitchens are far from ideal, unless there is the opportunity to link them with an adjoining living or dining area.

The overall style of kitchen can be modern or country, but uppermost in your mind must be the need to ensure that children can play in safety while adults cook. When planning the space, a good solution for harmonious relations is to make a designated area for children – include a child-size table and chairs, a soft play area, a toy box, space for books and games, a television or computer.

The layout of the kitchen should make it possible to keep an eye on children while also keeping dangerous or heavy kitchen items well out of reach. It may be necessary to include locked cupboards. Remember also that children love to help with tasks in the kitchen, so perhaps add a chair or steps so that they can reach the work surface to roll pastry or play in the sink.

All surfaces need to be tough and simple to wipe clean. Floors must be easy to mop or brush: linoleum, vinyl, wood with a tough varnish finish, sealed stone and ceramic are all good as flooring materials. The same goes for units: doors with lots of detail and ledges will collect dust and food, so sheer finishes are preferable. Incorporate rounded corners where possible, particularly at child's eye level.

Children love colourful environments, so you can be as wild as you like with the scheme. For a restrained effect, paint just one or two walls in bright colours, or add colour in the form of accessories or furniture. Good electric lighting is crucial, and should allow you to switch from bright lights at children's teatime to a subtle effect for entertaining.

Above The use of bold colours and attention to detail make family-friendly kitchens enjoyable places to be. The upside-down-teacup lampshade can't fail to raise a smile; robust old chairs and fruit boxes are painted different colours for a new lease of life; and pots and pans are festooned with jolly garlands.

Left Children automatically mean greater wear and tear on the home, so durable finishes such as extra-tough varnish used on wood floors and cupboards are essential for keeping the place looking smart.

Opposite A dining-room-cum-kitchen arrangement is ideal for families with children. A robust kitchen table doubles as a desk for homework, while long benches allow everyone to squeeze in at mealtimes.

Make a **play area** for children with a toy box, books and child-size **table and chairs**.

Incorporate a chair or steps that reach up to the work surface so **little hands can learn and help with the cooking**.

Add a splash of **colour and fun details** such as blackboards.

thoughtful design ...

Durable, wipe-clean surfaces, such as **wood flooring with a tough varnish finish**, vinyl or linoleum, are indispensable.

Good kitchen design **avoids sharp corners**, and keeps sharp, heavy and hot objects **out of children's reach**.

Flexible lighting lets you switch easily from a kids' tea to a **sophisticated supper**.

with space and interest for everyone

bedrooms

elements

planning the space

Making a plan sounds dull – the sort of thing your Mum
might nag you to do, or your teacher might tell you off for
not doing. Most of us want quick results. However, as with so
many tasks in life, groundwork pays off. Unless you live in a
house with plenty of generously proportioned rooms, your
bedroom will have to fulfil more than one role. As well as
being somewhere to retreat for intimacy, privacy, rest and
sleep, it will probably have to house clothes, shoes and bags.
It may also be the only reliably quiet place in a busy family
home and therefore the room where you choose to work.

Above The sleeping platform is a neat solution to separating a bedroom area in a one-room flat.

Left With meticulous planning and careful choice of furniture, working and sleeping spaces can be elegantly combined.

Opposite, left Storage units and a bed line two sides of this small bedroom. Books and toys are accessible on open shelves, while clothes and more toys are tucked away in cupboards. All in all, it is a recipe for that rare thing – a child's bedroom that is easy to keep tidy.

Opposite, right A curtained landing has been ingeniously utilized as impromptu guest accommodation.

- The most important piece of furniture is the bed. Decide on its **size and style first**. This is the starting point of your plan.

- Fitted furniture is almost always **a more efficient use of space** than unfitted furniture.

- Some fitted wardrobes are designed to make **an alcove for the bed**. This is an effective way to ensure that a wardrobe does not dominate a room.

- Clothes will be the main **storage issue**. Measure roughly how much **hanging space you need** before acquiring a wardrobe. Be generous.

Left Both space-saving and ideal for games, bunk beds remain a perennial favourite with children.
Below The steeply sloping ceiling of a bedroom in the roof is charming, but the arrangement of furniture needs careful consideration in order to minimize bumps on the head.
Opposite Space is a glorious luxury, here emphasized by the expanse of polished wooden floor and the lack of curtains at the tall casement windows. The design of a large room needs just as much care as a small one, but perhaps not quite as much cunning.

Space is always an issue in a bedroom. Usually, the problem is lack of space: how to fit in enough storage around the bed and still leave sufficient elbow-room to get dressed without having to stand on it.

In a small room there may be only one obvious place to put the bed – but using every scrap of available wall, floor and underneath space takes a bit more thought and ingenuity. You don't necessarily need to get out the graph paper and tape measure, although it can help, but you do need to sit and think about what goes where before you buy a giant wardrobe or even a small bedside table; fitted wardrobes might result in a better use of space, and your bedside table might need to double as a desk.

Think about lighting and where you will need to position it. Consider where you would like the radiator (it is not usually difficult or particularly expensive to relocate a radiator). And don't forget the space that is taken up by wardrobe doors when they are open or drawers when they are pulled out.

colour schemes

The traditional wisdom when choosing a colour scheme for a bedroom is to favour colours considered to be gentle, soothing and therefore sleep-inducing: pastels, creams, off-whites and neutrals. But colour is deeply subjective. While crisp, white linen certainly has the advantage of looking invitingly clean, there is no reason why the remainder of the decor should follow suit. A bedroom is essentially a private space and can be the arena in which to express entirely personal taste.

Above Chaste white walls are strongly contrasted with the rich strawberry red of bed linen and the strong purple of the bedside shelf. The effect is simple and dramatic.
Left Pastels, traditionally thought to be the most suitable colours for a bedroom, are used here to elegant effect.
Opposite The snowy bed linen in this theatrical room looks whiter than white in contrast with the scarlet of the walls, the purple suede of the headboard and the midnight-black background of the mural above.

It is difficult to prove, but nevertheless generally accepted, that colours can directly affect the emotions. However, the rules are far from universal. After all, who can say what the colour that you see as red looks like to anyone else? Of all the rooms in the home, your bedroom should be the one where you feel most free to indulge in the red that warms your heart, the blue that makes you smile.

Another, less personal aspect of colour is its ability to create certain optical effects. Pale and receding colours from the blue and green side of the colour spectrum tend to make spaces expand, while warm, 'advancing' colours – ranging from red through orange to yellow – pull walls in around the observer.

For creating a sense of spaciousness and increasing light, you cannot beat that most popular and innocuous of non-colours, white. But an all-white scheme can be too dazzling and clinical for a room in which you want to feel cocooned.

Instead, you can use white walls, or a more forgiving off-white, as the blank canvas on which to superimpose other favourite colours, whether you are making sharp contrasts with bright, strong shades or creating a subtler effect with paler, faded or neutral tones.

The advantage of a white, or near-white, background is that you can ring the changes when you tire of a particular colour scheme. You might even want to introduce a winter and summer palette – with darker, warmer curtains, bedspread, cushions and rugs to make you feel cosy on icy mornings replaced by gentle pastels for spring and summer.

In recent years the fashion has been for plain fabrics and wall treatments. This ought

Opposite, left Red is a rich, positive hue, especially those reds that are closer to purple than orange. Pale pink diaphanous curtains tone well with this shade of red, and the soft textures of the cushions and wall hanging make the bed look inviting.
Opposite, above right A striped quilt pulls together the colour scheme in this sophisticated bedroom.

Opposite, below right The honey-brown hue of natural wood brings warmth to a room distinctive for its clean, contemporary lines.
Above A pale terracotta wall paint complements the golden tones of a headboard and integral drawers.
Right Different shades of blue give this room a dreamy quality, ideal for rest and relaxation.

to make dealing with colour more straightforward. In fact, if everything from the floor covering to the curtains is a single colour, particular care must be given to the balance between these different shades and to the way they interact with one another. The latter is more difficult to predict than you might imagine. Simply holding a piece of fabric against a paint chart never tells the whole story. In this situation, a useful tool is a colour board – a pinboard to which you can attach samples of fabric, carpet and paint to see how well they coexist. The larger the samples and expanses of paint, the more accurately you will be able to predict the finished effect.

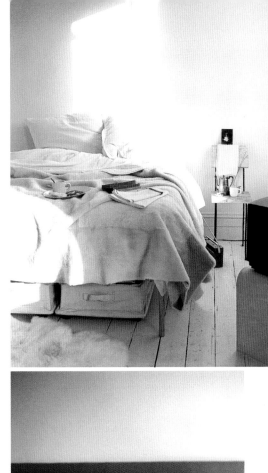

Above A disciplined colour scheme gives a room a certain element of formality as well as a sense of deep calm. The very strong contrast in this room between the dark walls, headboard and pillow borders and the bright white paintwork and bedspread is mitigated by the mid-tone of the natural wooden floor.

Above right Neutral tones have a more relaxed feel because there is less play on contrast.

Right and opposite The effects of contrast are softened in this room, which draws from a palette of whites, off-whites and soft grey. Texture adds both visual and tactile interest to a study in monochrome.

- A **flourish of pattern** in a room dominated by plains can add **coherence** to a colour scheme – for example, **a faded chintz** that brings together the pale wood of the floorboards and the lilac of the walls, or **a multi-coloured stripe** that links more contrasting shades.

- Paint **a large piece of cardboard** with the shade of paint you are considering and prop it against **all the walls** of the room in turn. It won't look **quite the same** in one position as in another.

- Colours vary depending on **how they are lit**. A bedroom colour should look good in artificial and **natural light**.

Below Apart from the bed, storage is the most important element of the furnishings in any bedroom. Fitted wardrobes are an extremely efficient use of space and, as here, can combine sections for hanging and folding as well as that bedroom essential, a full-length mirror. There are many excellent modular ranges that can be purchased off the peg and put together to suit personal requirements, and these tend to be less expensive than commissioning bespoke joinery.

Above The style of bed you choose will be the key to the decoration of the room. Here the feel is robust and almost industrial: a metal bedstead, which uses poles and connectors reminiscent of scaffolding, sheltering under a metal spiral staircase, which may once have been a fire escape.

Opposite A completely plain low divan, dressed in white, evokes a mood of meditative simplicity – an effect reinforced by the restrained, almost monastic architecture of the room.

furniture & storage

Whether it is a modern divan or an antique extravaganza, the bed remains the central feature of any bedroom, and is likely to be the single most expensive item of furniture in the room. While a bed's appearance will set the style for the decor, its comfort is equally important. Choosing the right mattress is not simply a question of ensuring a good night's sleep; it can also prevent back problems. If you prefer a soft mattress, choose a bed with a sprung divan base. Mattresses suitable for laying on wooden slats tend to be much firmer. Whatever kind of mattress you invest in, remember to turn it a couple of times a year to keep the wear evenly spread.

Antique bedsteads can be irresistibly beautiful but apparently impractical, since they are rarely a standard size – Victorian double beds, for example, are often far too narrow to satisfy modern notions of king-sized comfort. However, a Victorian double bed can make a pleasantly generous 21st-century single and, even if you cannot find a duvet of exactly the right size, there are companies which will make a bespoke mattress to fit an old bed frame for a price that compares favourably with a good-quality standard mattress.

Second only in importance to the bed is storage. Most of us lack a separate dressing-room or a walk-in wardrobe, so somewhere to keep clothes fresh and free of dust must be found in the bedroom itself. Never before have so many people owned so many clothes. Where once a few hooks and a wooden chest would have sufficed, we now require ranks of drawers, tiers of shoe racks and metres of hanging rail.

Opposite, left Sleeping space in this loft conversion can be set up almost anywhere. All it takes is a couple of tatami mats, futons and pillows.

Left and below A stylish bedhead gives presence to a simple divan. The plain upholstered bedhead (left) looks neat and contemporary, while the huge piece of roughly carved wood (below) seems to shelter the bed as well as adding character.

Right and far right, top and middle Carefully laundered and folded bed linen offers an aesthetic pleasure.

Far right, bottom A bedside table should be large enough to hold books and a glass of water.

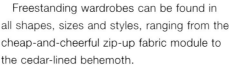

Freestanding wardrobes can be found in all shapes, sizes and styles, ranging from the cheap-and-cheerful zip-up fabric module to the cedar-lined behemoth.

Similarly, chests and chests-of-drawers can be anything from valuable antiques to basic items made of painted MDF. Antique pieces are not necessarily more expensive than good-quality new furniture, but wardrobes that predate 1900 tend to be too narrow for modern coat-hangers. And don't buy an old wardrobe or chest that smells of mothballs – or your clothes will ever afterwards smell like great-grandmother's attic.

A large bedroom can accommodate freestanding wardrobes and chests, but in small rooms fitted cupboards will give you a lot more volume per square metre of floor space. Fitted cupboards can reach right up

to the ceiling and into corners and alcoves. You can install fitted cupboards along a whole wall, or design them to flank the bed with high cupboards across the top, making a recess into which the bedhead fits. The inevitable consequence of this is that some cupboards are more easily accessible than others, and you will probably find that a certain amount of juggling is a biannual necessity – packing summer clothes into boxes banished to high cupboards in the winter and doing the same with bulky woollens in the summer.

Labelling boxes in which you keep things for infrequent use can save a lot of time and rummaging. A Polaroid photograph attached to the front of stacked boxes of shoes provides a neat form of quick identification.

Once you have somewhere to lay your head and hang your jacket, additional furnishings are more a question of space and choice than necessity. At the top of the list should be a bedside table, providing an invaluable surface for a reading

Opposite, above left A wood-panelled bedroom is enriched by examples of design icons of the 20th century: an undulating screen by Charles Eames and a leather upholstered chaise by Edward Wormley.

Opposite, above right An antique wooden chest, probably designed to hold documents, looks entirely at home in a modern bedroom, while its shallow drawers make ideal storage for socks, pants, ties and other small items of clothing.

Opposite, below Bespoke storage, like this sleek wall of cupboards and drawers, can be designed exactly to suit requirements, giving the right mixture of hanging space, shelf space and drawer space.

Above A decorative feature has been made of the storage in this Shaker-style bedroom. Ranks of drawers have been fitted into a recess where you might expect to see cupboards. Dotted with the dark spots of their handles, they create a pleasing geometry, but remembering what is kept in each of them must be a daily challenge.

Left and far left Strikingly modern cupboards make a bold statement in the bedroom of this otherwise traditionally furnished period house. The deep doors contain extra storage and swing open to reveal hanging space and open drawers.

light, book, alarm clock and glass of water. Even a little corner shelf can save you having to fumble under the bed to find a tissue or turn off the beeping at 7a.m. sharp. If there is room for only one other item of furniture, it should probably be a chair – not just for sitting on to do up your shoes or paint your toenails but as somewhere to drape a throw or leave your clothes overnight.

If you still have empty floor space, you can add more furnishings, either useful pieces, such as a small desk, or primarily decorative ones, such as a pretty screen or indulgent chaise longue. Soft furnishings in a bedroom give it the feel of a boudoir – a haven to which you might retreat in the middle of the day, not only when you are ready for bed.

Above A modern interpretation of the Shaker fitted drawers, these deep square drawers are ideal for bulky jumpers and jeans.

Left Box shelving in a young child's bedroom can be used for books, toys and games. Artfully arranged, it looks attractive, too.

Far left A bedside table with a cupboard and drawer is doubly useful. The extra storage means that you can afford to leave its top uncluttered.

Opposite A bedhead that is deep enough to be used as a shelf is a sleek alternative to a bedside table.

- **Parkinson's Law** applies to storage just as surely as to so many other aspects of life: however much you have, **you will surely fill it**.

- Don't forget the **dead space beneath the bed**. Some beds are designed to incorporate drawers; alternatively, boxes can hold a surprising amount concealed beneath **the overhang of a bedspread**.

- **Foldaway beds** used to require two strong men to raise and lower them. Modern versions are **elegant in looks** and operation and give you daytime **floor space** that would otherwise be unusable.

- A **full-length mirror** is essential not only for reasons of vanity; judiciously placed, it can also increase the **sense of space and light**.

window treatments
& soft furnishings

The softness and texture of fabrics are essential to the comfort of a bedroom. Just as the bed would be painfully unwelcoming without its sheets and blankets or duvet, an unadorned bedroom window can leave you feeling exposed and unsafe. Not that it is necessary to have acres of billowing fabric. Slatted shutters or blinds might suit your room better. But the style of window treatment you choose will not only be a question of looks; it will also depend on how much light you wish to exclude and how much privacy you need to gain.

Top These attractive sash windows might have been swamped by curtains. Instead, the owners have chosen blackout roller blinds, which disappear when not in use.
Above Thick woollen curtains provide a protective shield for a bed with its back to the windows.
Right A bold gingham contrasted with airy white voile makes curtains that are both functional and pretty.
Opposite A wall of windows in this sun-flooded room is veiled by sheer cotton. The folds of fabric filter the glare and soften the feel of the space.

Sometimes the only way to achieve the look you want, and make it practical, is to use a combination of fabrics or fabrics and blinds.

White blackout blinds are a very effective means of cutting out light and can be used alone for a minimal look; tucked inside the window embrasure, they barely show at all. However, for daytime privacy, you may want to add a layer of sheer curtain.

If you would also like to minimize draughts and muffle noise, you can add yet another layer to your window treatment with heavy, lined curtains on top of the sheers – not quite as effective as double glazing, but possibly less expensive.

Once you have decided what you require in terms of function, you can enjoy playing with the aesthetics of your windows. Curtains, whether traditional chintz or crumpled linen, are the most feminine option and tend to make a room feel cosy and cut off from the outside world. Blinds, whether roman, roller or venetian, have a crisper, cooler look and take up less floor and wall space.

Like curtains, soft furnishings in a bedroom have a cocooning effect. If you have enough floor space for a squashy armchair, a chaise longue or even a sofa, this is a sure way to make your bedroom an irresistible haven at any time of the day. A chaise longue is particularly appropriate – a piece of furniture specially designed for lazy lounging, ideal for those times when you don't feel ready for bed but would rather recline than sit up.

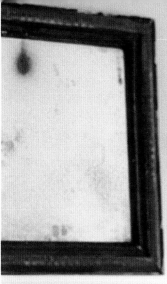

- **Unbleached linen scrim** makes a cheap but stylish sheer, and **old linen sheets**, lined or unlined, look fresh and surprisingly modern.

- A **contrasting lining** or a wide band of fabric along the leading edges or the base will **make your curtains unique**. Aim for an interesting mix.

- Giving a more architectural look than curtains or blinds, **well-fitting shutters** provide good insulation against light, noise and weather.

- If you lack space for a sofa, you may be able to squeeze in **a small padded ottoman**, providing a place to sit and extra storage.

Above Vintage quilts add an extra layer of warmth to a bed as well as introducing the charm of faded florals.
Right Modern luxury takes the form of a silk-lined throw.
Opposite, above left A generous armchair with matching stool is an invitation to sit with your feet up.
Opposite, above right Draped over the arm of a chair or the end of a bed, a downy throw represents the perfect accessory for bedroom lounging.
Opposite, below The chaise longue is a piece of furniture specifically designed for resting out of bed and makes an elegant addition to any bedroom.

lighting & display

As any film star will tell you, the difference between good and bad lighting reflects the distinction between flattery and the unvarnished truth. Even the prettiest room is ruined by a harsh overhead light; better to have several ceiling spots, supplemented by table lamps. Bedroom lights should ideally be on a dimmer switch; otherwise, a choice of independent light sources allows you to control the illumination intensity. A strong light is desirable for checking your appearance in the mirror, but otherwise, in a room where you want to feel relaxed, softer lighting is more appropriate. Good directional reading lights are essential if you want to avoid eye strain.

Left A wall light beside the bed leaves more surface space to put things on; in this instance, there is room for a decorative glass bottle.
Far left The source of light from a bedside illumination should be above the reader's eye level, as in the case of this elegant table lamp.
Below Several different light sources allow maximum flexibility. The paper globe shade softens and diffuses the overhead lighting.
Opposite The simple lines and jaunty angle of a vintage lamp give it a strong presence in a modern bedroom. Its height and position just behind the reader are ideal for comfortable reading.

The right level of artificial light in a room can profoundly affect your comfort, as well as showing the room off at its most attractive.

While some types of light such as recessed spotlights are designed to be unobtrusive, other types can be decorative features in themselves. Obviously, function should take precedence over form – a stunning bedside lamp that gives out a faint green glow is a waste of space. However, given the huge choice of lighting now available, there is no reason why a light that does the job it is designed for should not also look good.

The only exception to the function-before-form rule applies to chandeliers, which may emit a light that is neither pleasing nor useful, but nonetheless make beautiful decorative mobiles hanging from the ceiling.

Closely linked with lighting is display, perhaps the most personal element of any room. As your bedroom is likely to be the space in the home that is least on show, you can please yourself with little decorative flourishes. This might be the place for your collection of handbags or glass candlesticks, for example. To avoid a cluttered look, group collections of things together. A wall of photographs, all in similar frames, looks less untidy than individual photographs scattered around the room propped on every available surface.

Top left A choice of lettering from old shop signs, arranged according to colour and font as opposed to sense, makes a quirky and amusing display on a bedroom wall.
Left A passion for red shoes is on show in this all-white bedroom with its specially designed shelves.

Above Deep suspended shelves in a child's bedroom make books the subject of an attractive display.
Right Where there is no space for a bedside table, as in this room, a wall light is the obvious solution, its switch conveniently positioned just above the pillow.

- Wall lights are **great space savers** and can be positioned above a bed at whatever height you find most **comfortable for reading**.

- The light from a table lamp is directed and coloured by its shade. A **pale parchment shade** gives a soft and diffused light.

- Bedrooms are private enough to allow a bit of decorative nostalgia, whether it is the moth-eaten rabbit you slept with as a child or your **favourite wedding photograph**.

- If you cannot afford curtains **in a fabric you love**, buy a single length of it and hang it from **a pole on the wall** behind your bed.

bedrooms

styles

contemporary

Minimalism in its extreme form is difficult for most people to live with. A less demanding version of the style achieves its effects with clean lines, plain surfaces and streamlined modern furnishings – for interiors with a calm, contemporary feel. If you want to create this look in a bedroom, it is essential to have ample and efficient storage.

Above Natural materials, such as the wood panelling behind this bed, play a vital part in humanizing the streamlined interior. Simple, sheer curtains filter the light and make a pleasing contrast with the smooth gloss of the wood.
Right The balance between areas of plain colour is well judged in this elegant room. The hugely enlarged photograph of a flower adds a striking dash of pattern and some organic curves.
Opposite The straight lines in this neat, stylish room are offset by textured fabrics. In addition to the deeply corded carpet, heavy bedspread and matching cushions, a slightly padded fabric has been used to panel the walls around the bed, making a cleverly integral bedhead.

The contemporary style is ideal for people who enjoy the discipline of perfect tidiness. A plain modern divan dressed with crisp white bed linen, a simple bedside table and lamp, white walls, roller blinds – and there you have the essential ingredients of a contemporary-style bedroom. But the effect is easily ruined by, say, a clutter of shoes, discarded clothes or piles of magazines. Everything extraneous needs to be hidden away, ideally behind a wall of sleek cupboard doors.

However, as the pictures on these pages show, to make a room that is both simple and beautiful is a subtle and complicated business. Where you have only a few pieces, it is worth buying the best quality you can afford. The emptier and plainer a room, the more care needs to be taken over balance and contrast, whether between blocks of

Left This small bedroom, sectioned off from a larger room by a sliding door, has been pared down to the essentials. It finds its character in a sculptural armchair, a compelling piece of wall art and the sloping ceiling with hidden light source.

Above A streamlined, empty look is far easier to achieve when you have an expanse of floor space to play with. Sticking to a very limited palette of colours also helps. In this room, bright white has been used to contrast with natural wood.

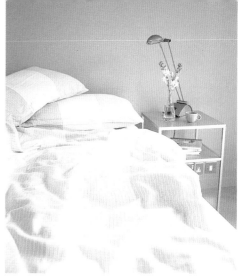

Left and above Painting a wooden floor in a satin-finish floor paint creates a good-looking, durable surface that is plain and relatively inexpensive. The smoky blue-grey used on the floor and walls of this room gives it an almost ethereal quality, as if the bed, with its matching blue-striped linen, were floating in a bubble of colour. **Below** The less clutter and colour a room contains, the more noticeable texture and shape become.

colour, or shapes of furniture. For example, pairing a low bed with a tall cupboard can produce a dramatic effect. If the palette is limited to only a few colours, or to shades that are very similar to one another, then different textures are vital in order to provide visual, as well as tactile, variety.

Care must also be taken to ensure that a bedroom in the contemporary style does not feel too hard-edged. Where straight lines predominate, a curve or two will introduce variety of line, just as texture breaks the monotony of colour. Use natural materials such as glossy wood, heavy linen and soft cashmere to offset an impression of austerity. Often the plump mounds of pillows and the soft drape of a bedspread will be enough to counteract the effect of too many right angles.

plain colours, clean lines ...

When less means more in an interior style, **quality matters**. Buy the best you can afford, particularly when it comes to **bed linen and flooring**.

Very plain rooms can give an austere impression. **Use natural materials** to convey a feeling of luxury.

and no clutter

Be disciplined about tidiness and **make sure everything has a home**, from shoes and bags to boxes of paper tissues.

Use **balance and contrast** – for example, match a wall of dark wood with a wall of white curtain, a polished concrete floor with **a sheepskin rug**.

Right The exposed wooden framework of this country cottage has been augmented to make simple bunk beds. Clothes hang on pegs, as they did before the advent of the clothes hanger.

Below A floral quilt and a quaint antique lamp provide old-fashioned comfort and convenience.

Opposite New owners have left the interior walls of this 16th-century house almost untouched, with layers of limewash and scraps of wallpaper telling their own story about the history of its decoration. The antique furnishings also have a patina of age and look comfortably at home in their well-worn setting.

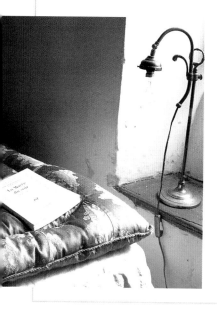

country

Country style can be re-created anywhere from a cottage in a field to the interior of a suburban semi. Its essence is a relaxed, quiet nostalgia, and while beams, inglenooks and uneven walls all add to the charm, they are not essential. Above all, this is a style that allows for the shabby and the quirky alongside simple, traditional furnishings and fabrics.

A country-style bed can be anything from a plain four-poster to a metal bedstead, as long as it is not too grand. An antique will have the patina acquired from years of wear and tear, but there are plenty of good reproduction versions to be found. Add an old-fashioned bedspread over the duvet, or rediscover the pleasures of sheets and blankets. Genuine antique quilts are expensive and often too fragile for daily use, but feather-filled eiderdowns from our grandmothers' era are easy to find in antique shops and market stalls, and make a pretty addition to any bed (shake them well before you buy just to make sure they are not losing too many feathers).

Since the country look is far from streamlined, it is worth considering freestanding as opposed to fitted storage. Old French armoires are particularly capacious, and antique chests-of-drawers – popular bedroom furnishings for more than 200 years – are plentiful. Good-quality chests-of-drawers are expensive, but you can always find something tatty and do it up yourself. In fact, expensive woods such as mahogany and rosewood don't tend to fit with the country look, which favours cheaper pine or painted furniture, preferably pieces

Left Panelling a room with painted match-boarding gives it instant country charm.
Below Cotton ticking, originally designed for use as mattress and pillow covers, is far too good to hide.
Bottom The contrast of textures between the slightly rough woollen blanket and the smooth cotton sheets make this bed look particularly inviting.
Opposite, above left The extra-large squares give this patchwork quilt a modern twist.
Opposite, below left and right Examples of recycling range from painted metal bedsteads from a school dormitory to a new bag made from old French table linen.

that are a bit chipped and rubbed. Wicker hampers and wooden chests make good storage for spare sheets and blankets or clothes that are out of season.

When looking for fabrics, choose traditional designs in cotton and linen; silks, velvets and damasks are too opulent for this homespun style. Ginghams, floral chintzes, floral sprigs and striped tickings all have the right look and feel. If you want to keep the effect really simple, stick to checks or stripes. For a more feminine look, mix in faded florals and monochrome toiles. A rose-scattered curtain trimmed with a border of checked gingham or a striped valance under a toile bedspread looks pretty as a picture.

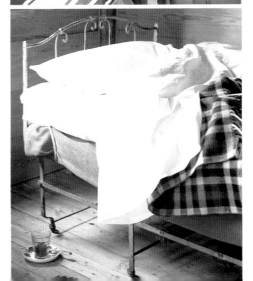

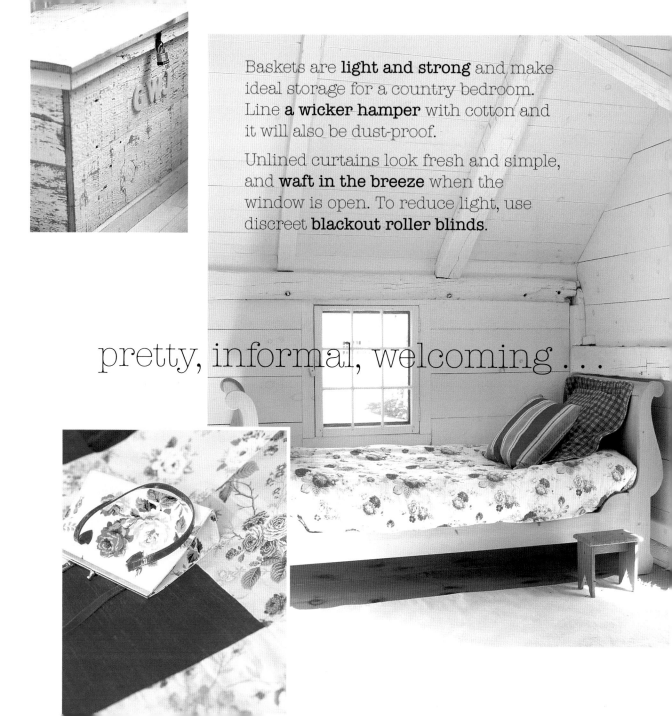

Baskets are **light and strong** and make ideal storage for a country bedroom. Line **a wicker hamper** with cotton and it will also be dust-proof.

Unlined curtains look fresh and simple, and **waft in the breeze** when the window is open. To reduce light, use discreet **blackout roller blinds**.

pretty, informal, welcoming . . .

Fresh flowers – whether **cow parsley in a milk bottle** or garden roses in a glass jug – add beauty and **the scent of outdoors.**

Wooden floorboards and cotton rugs have **the right rustic feel**, or choose one of the natural mattings **such as coir or seagrass.**

a restful room

classically elegant

Classical style, derived from Greek and Roman architecture, has been endlessly revived and reworked, adapted to suit 18th-century stately homes and 20th-century town halls. In its purest form it has been the preserve of the rich and powerful. But humbler, more accessible versions of classical style can also be seen in urban terraces and village houses.

Left The character of this room is defined by an imposing antique French bed, its dark wood and curvaceous carvings outlined against pure white walls. Barely-there curtains and the lack of any other decoration ensure that the bed is the unchallenged focus.

Below This painted chair with its cane seat and back is a copy of an 18th-century design.

Opposite A single piece of furniture can give a room a classical feel. In this bedroom, the piece is an unusual antique cupboard with arched doors flanked by pillars. The restrained colour scheme of white and lilac enhances the impression of refinement.

The classically elegant style is sophisticated and serene. Just as people who are tall and slim generally find it easier to dress elegantly, so it is a great advantage, if your chosen style is 'classical', to have rooms with high ceilings. Tall beds, long curtains, high cupboards – all are practical impossibilities unless you have at least two and a half vertical metres to play with. So this style is unlikely to be the best choice for a country cottage or an urban basement. However, many small city flats have been converted from houses that were once quite grand, and these spaces, with their typically tall windows, are well suited to classical elegance.

Height is important not only architecturally; a room furnished with a low divan, a low chest and nothing that reaches towards the ceiling lacks the necessary formality. A slim four-poster is ideal, perhaps draped with sheer, white cotton or left bare for a more austere look. Well-chosen antiques, whether a single chair or a set of architectural prints, will add to the understated glamour.

Fabrics can be luxurious silks and velvets, if you can afford them, but you will achieve a more tranquil effect by keeping colours plain. Stripes in two colours have a strongly classical feel. Cheap cotton ticking, lined and made up into full-length curtains, can look surprisingly stately. If you want to introduce more pattern, choose a monochrome toile, but don't use too much of it or the room will start to take on a country feel.

Right Painted the colour of clotted cream, this French bedhead is as timelessly chic as a pale linen suit.
Far right Antiques don't have to be opulent to be graceful, as this bentwood chair perfectly illustrates.
Below The tall, tapered posts of the bed and its Shaker-style simplicity set the tone in a room that is both contemporary and classical.
Opposite, above left and right Rooms furnished with antiques often have a soothing sense of permanence – one of the characteristics of the English country house style.
Opposite, below The tall, slim, metal four-poster and the specially made cupboard in this bedroom are obviously modern, even though the design of both borrows ideas from antique furniture.

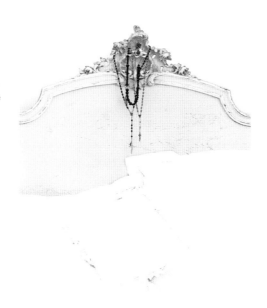

A large **mosquito net** makes an attractive and inexpensive bed canopy, adding **presence and height** to a simple divan.

A colour scheme made up of whites, off-whites and shades of cream is a **recipe for sophistication**.

cool, refined....

Make a ceiling look higher by painting walls with **wide vertical stripes** in different shades of the same colour.

Well-framed photocopies make a surprisingly **convincing substitute for antique prints.** Hang them in a group for maximum impact.

Give fitted cupboards panelled doors - it will make them look **more architectural.**

traditional and sophisticated

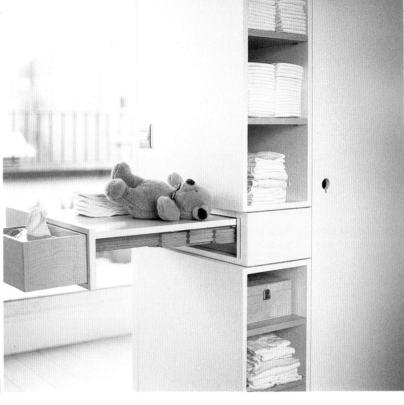

Right This nursery storage unit was specially built by a carpenter. The cupboard has a pull-out changing surface and a box to hold baby wipes, plus shelves for nappies.
Opposite If you combine proper cupboard storage with easy-access shelves, toddlers can easily get hold of their favourite things.
Below Scaled-down furniture is a friendly as well as a practical part of a toddler's bedroom.

children's rooms

Babies have few requirements when it comes to bedroom furniture, but as children grow their needs change – and change again. Adopt a five-year plan, and anticipate each new need, from a work desk to funky furnishings for pre-teens. The bed may be the top priority in a child's room, but storage comes a close second. Not everything has to be put away at all times, but each item should have a home.

Below right A Victorian day bed, with decorative open ironwork, makes an attractive bed choice for older girls. It looks particularly romantic draped with a fabric canopy or mosquito net.

Below Girls love to admire their clothes, so provide space to line up shoes, plus low hooks for hanging up hats and party dresses.

When a toddler turns two and graduates from a cot to a bed, it provides a timely moment for reassessing the bedroom and making stylistic changes. Focus first on the hard-working furniture, planning colours later. Invest in the best mattress you can afford. Children may be light but they need firm support, and a good-quality mattress should last for ten years. Think long and hard about the style of bed you choose. Girls will go through myriad fads, from Barbie-doll fever at five to seriously sophisticated at ten. Work backwards. If a classic style with a contemporary twist seems suitable for a pre-teen, it can be made appropriately childlike for the earlier years.

Canopied and four-poster beds, bunk beds or sleeping platforms prove irresistible to girls, as well as providing extra space for sleepover friends. A simple wood or tubular metal four-poster offers plenty of decorative potential. For example, frames can be draped with brightly coloured net or, for older girls, with inexpensive, glittery sari silks.

If the room is big enough, the smartest and simplest storage solution is to install a run of cupboards with floor-to-ceiling, flush-fitting doors along one wall. This façade can conceal a multitude of different-sized shelves, roomy enough to hold individual crates for small items yet deep enough for piles of sweaters and jeans, and including space for a hanging rail.

Above and above left A metal bedstead is a good investment, since it can be restyled from year to year or resprayed in a new colour. Search junk shops for antique versions. A headboard at each end has its advantages, providing somewhere to pile up pillows and to hang bags and toys. An older girl will appreciate plenty of open storage. Here, toys, schoolwork and treasures are all to hand.

In a boy's room, everything needs to be robust. Imagine each piece of furniture being climbed on, jumped off or moved around as part of a pirate ship game or impromptu kickabout, and you'll get a realistic picture. Pick scratch-resistant modern materials like laminate and plywood, or painted furniture that can be touched up with a lick of paint.

Boys still require a cosy sleeping nook at the age of three, but by five are ready for a more adventurous, classically boyish option. Either buy a generously sized cot bed for the baby stage and get a serious boy's bed once your son outgrows the cot or invest in a grown-up bed at the age of two, and make it inviting for the early years.

Boys, as much as girls, appreciate a fuss being made over their bed. From a child's point of view, a bed is not only somewhere to sleep but also a special secure zone, as well as being a potential platform for games. Ready-to-buy modern options include sophisticated dark wood or painted bateau-lit and sleigh-bed frames, simple iron bedsteads or colourful lacquered MDF platform beds with storage drawers. For most boys past the age of five, a bunk bed is a dream option. A number of shops now stock tubular metal bunk beds, which are infinitely more stylish than the varnished pine variety.

Most boys have little interest in putting clothes away, so devise a simple storage system. Open shelves in a cupboard

Left In this toddler's bedroom, a high picket-fence headboard, a faux-fur rug and thick, tufted curtains promote a safe, cosy feel.
Below Furniture on castors and bright plastic storage crates that can be slotted under the bed are invaluable in a small room.
Opposite, left As an alternative to dog-eared posters, consider a bold painted canvas depicting your son's favourite sporting hero.
Opposite, right Brilliant, saturated colour on every surface turns an ordinary bedroom into an exciting playroom. Here, the startling walls are matched by equally vibrant bed linen – a riot of crazy stripes, animals and exotic fruit.

are the easiest option, but clearly label each section for T-shirts, jeans and so on. Alternatively, build a series of box-shaped cupboards at child height all around the room, with each one devoted to a certain category of clothing, and fitted with a different-coloured MDF or stainless-steel door to resemble a sports locker.

Give boys a chance to create their own ambience in the room using lighting – a bubble lamp by the bed, a light-up globe on the desk or a funky coil of lights are all good options. Try to squeeze in a few quirky additions. A football table, punchbag or wall-hung basketball hoop will make your son's room the coolest den he could ask for.

a bedroom is ...

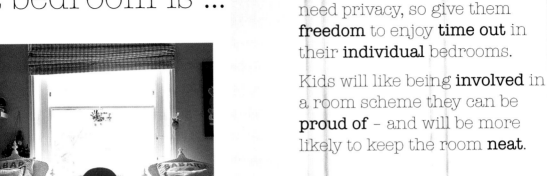

Children, just like **adults**, need privacy, so give them **freedom** to enjoy **time out** in their **individual** bedrooms.

Kids will like being **involved** in a room scheme they can be **proud of** – and will be more likely to keep the room **neat**.

a child's private space

Plan bedrooms that are fun for **little friends**, with seating to chill out on, or a futon for **sleepovers**.

Adopt a five-year plan, and anticipate each **new** need, from a work desk to **funky furnishings** for pre-teens.

bathrooms

elements

planning the space

The most efficient way to begin the planning process is to define the role of your new bathroom. Will it be an ensuite or family bathroom? Is it likely to be used by more than one person at a time? Will any of those using the bathroom be very young or old and infirm? Do you want it to double as a dressing room? Do you like to bathe quickly or in a leisurely way? Do you need storage only for toiletries or for towels and cleaning products as well? Think about style, too. Do you favour a contemporary or traditional look? Does the design need to integrate with an adjoining room? The answers to these questions and others like them will help you to decide your priorities.

Above This narrow corridor of a bathroom relies on glass, mirror and dramatic lighting to push back its boundaries. The working area is defined by its pale limestone wall and floor, and clear-glass partitions separate the zones of activity.

Left A custom-made shower makes clever use of a confined space in this tiny internal bathroom. The curved shape eliminates the need for a shower door and its glass brick construction allows light to enter from an adjoining room.

Opposite, left and right This long, narrow bathroom has been made into a visually squarer, more comfortable space by fitting a shower cubicle across one end wall and building the bath into a raised platform at the other. Light emanating from above and below the wall behind the basin focuses attention at the centre of the room and adds to the impression of greater width.

The basic fixtures for a conventional bathroom are a basin, lavatory and bath, but there are many variations, and your choice will depend on the style you want, your budget and the size of your room. In a small bathroom, the tub could be exchanged for a shower enclosure to save space – or, for a feeling of openness, the room could be designed as a fully waterproofed wet-room. If you want both a bath and shower, the choice is between separate fittings or an overbath shower. In some countries, every well-appointed bathroom contains a bidet, while in others it is an optional extra. Generally, top-quality fittings with designer labels are expensive, but there are plenty of good-looking alternatives in affordable ranges.

To see whether your fixtures will fit into the available space, draw a scale floor plan of the room and elevations of each wall on graph paper, then cut out cardboard shapes representing the fixtures to the same scale (manufacturers' brochures give exact sizes). On the floor plan and elevations, mark all permanent features such as windows and doorways, and place the cutouts on the plan, moving them around to find a feasible layout. Baths need a strip at least 90cm (36in) wide beside them to allow bathers to step out and dry themselves; showers need a space 70cm (28in) wide. Basins require 70cm (28in) in front and 20cm (8in) at the sides; the lavatory and bidet need 60cm (24in) in front and 20cm (8in) at the sides. In a room used by one person at a time, access areas can be overlapped slightly, but bathrooms used by two or more people at once need extra space. While arranging the fixtures, refer to the elevations to identify any conflict with doors, windows or radiators. Doors can be re-hung or moved and radiators moved or replaced by underfloor heating to accommodate awkward layouts.

• Spend time getting your plans right. **Even small changes** like installing a shaver socket or an extractor fan **will be disruptive** if they are made later.

• Fixtures and fittings come in **many shapes and sizes**; if you are planning a small or awkwardly shaped room, look at as many brochures as you can.

• If you want a chair, cabinet or other freestanding furniture in the room, allow for it **at the planning stage**.

• Pipework collects dirt and looks unsightly so **hide it behind boxed skirting boards**, false walls or some other form of ducting.

Above and left Open shelves and a console vanity unit leave the floor area in this bathroom uncluttered and easy to clean.
Opposite, above Designed for busy mornings, this compact shower room has a long basin that can be used by two people at the same time. A flanking wall screens an open shower enclosure from the door.
Opposite, below A false wall along one side of the room neatly conceals the cistern for a back-to-the-wall lavatory and the plumbing for a shower.

Above Thick tinted glass forms a sleek countertop with integral circular bowls. Super stylish, it is also practical, with no joints where dirt and limescale can lodge.

Right and opposite, left Visually as well as physically weighty, the grey-brown mussel limestone covering most of the surfaces in this room is offset by expanses of white. On the horizontal, the stone is polished to show off the subtleties of its colour and texture, but on the vertical planes it is has been given narrow, regular grooves for textural and tonal contrast.

Opposite, right This superior form of duck-boarding surrounding a sunken bath lets water drain through it.

surfaces, flooring & lighting

The floor and walls form the background against which fixtures, furniture and accessories are seen. Since they make up such a large part of the picture, the materials covering them have a major influence on the style of a room; similar or complementary materials are likely to be used for the countertops, bath surround and other hardworking surfaces. Bathrooms require two distinct types of lighting: general all-over illumination and task lighting.

The ideal flooring for a conventional bathroom is water-tolerant, easy to clean, slip-resistant and warm to the touch. Vinyl, rubber and cork possess all these qualities but tile, stone, glass, wood and even carpet are suitable floor coverings provided they are chosen and used with care. Hard materials such as tile, stone and glass are often used in modern settings, but they are cold and potentially slippery when wet.

Wood and carpet may be the least water-tolerant materials, but they are comfortable to walk on and look luxurious. Unless you choose the kind specifically designed for bathrooms, laminated wood flooring may swell and distort in a damp environment, and solid timber requires careful sealing to protect against splinters and watermarks. Duck-boarding and painted floorboards remain comparatively unscathed by water and can safely be used in adult bathrooms where the floor does not get too wet.

The range of wall treatments suitable for bathrooms is almost limitless provided the wet areas are properly protected. Continuous surfaces are often chosen for a contemporary scheme to give a sophisticated, seamless look, and for small spaces which appear all the more cramped if the walls are fragmented into a patchwork of textures and colours. Materials suitable for creating this all-over look include ceramic or glass tiles and mosaic and natural and synthetic stone, all of which are comparatively expensive but long-lasting,

Above Terracotta, hardwood, rubber and porcelain all make suitable flooring for wet areas. Terracotta tiles have a robust look and natural colour that warms country bathrooms; slatted timber is a top choice for a smart urban setting; resilient, colourful rubber is practical for a family bathroom; while porcelain offers a variety of size, shape and colour on a grand scale.
Opposite, left Softwood is not generally recommended for bathroom flooring but exposed floorboards, naturally ventilated from beneath and painted to protect against moisture, are serviceable and have a certain rustic charm. A cotton runner placed alongside the bath gives further protection from water.

Below Randomly arranged mosaic tiles, corrugated PVC roofing and sheet vinyl flooring are inexpensive surface elements that combine harmoniously to create a practical and colourful bathroom.

waterproof and easy to clean. In traditional bathrooms and lower-budget installations, paint and wallpaper are decorative options for all walls other than those in the shower enclosure; if a uniform look is required, surfaces immediately around the bath and basin can be protected with clear glass or acrylic panels or plain matching tiles.

Wood panelling is an option for the walls of both traditional and modern bathrooms. In the bathrooms of period or country homes, painted tongue-and-groove wainscoting or fielded panelling covering the lower part of the wall may be continued around the room; they will withstand normal levels of bathroom moisture though not the direct spray of a

Above Drawn from nature, the floor in this bathroom is made from beach pebbles set in concrete, while the wall is clad with the pale, blond stems of bamboo.
Left Inexpensive plywood tiles take on a glamorous look when laid diamond fashion and studded with 'key stones' of black-stained ply. Lacquer applied in several layers not only protects the wood from moisture but enhances its golden tones and gives it a satin sheen.

Right Dark, handsome and expensive, iroko wood panelling remains unblemished by water. Lightly oiled to maintain its rich colour, the timber gives the room a sense of luxury and permanence.

Far right Porcelain tiles, whose colour and texture recall polished limestone, form a waterproof panel that can be distinguished from the wall only by its reflectivity. The mosaic bath panel adds further surface interest but allows no colour to intrude on this neutral scheme.

Below The tough industrial aesthetic of concrete offers an interesting and unexpected contrast to sleek, domesticated materials such as lacquer and mirror glass. Custom-fabricated, it must be sealed before use.

shower. Natural or oiled hardwood, such as iroko or merbau, is the modern alternative. Dark tropical timbers resist water to a degree, but will fade if not regularly oiled.

Smooth, panelled surfaces are easier to clean than tiles or mosaic, which eventually accumulate grime in their grouted joints. The most popular of these are limestone, marble, granite, Corian and glass; in urban homes, industrial-style options such as concrete and sheet metals may be added to the list. All of these materials are hard-wearing, but extra care must be taken with limestone and marble which can be marked by cosmetics and acidic cleaners and badly damaged by cleaners that contain limescale remover.

As in other rooms in the home, the most satisfactory general light in a bathroom is provided by daylight. In most bathrooms, this can be maximized by keeping window treatments simple, but in windowless internal rooms more radical measures are needed, such as replacing sections of the wall with glass bricks or obscured glass panels to allow light from an adjoining room to pass through. After dark and on grey, wintry days, a central ceiling light, downlighters recessed into the ceiling or wall fittings give even all-over light, leaving no gloomy spots in the room.

Bathroom task lighting – for activities such as shaving and applying make-up – centres on the mirror and should be directed so that it shines on your face. A pair of lights placed at the sides of the mirror will give a clear, virtually shadow-free light; the light sources may either be separate wall-mounted fittings or incorporated into the mirror itself.

Above A curve of obscured glass separates a shower area from a living space. Its frosted finish diffuses, and maximizes, the light passing through.
Left This dark, concrete-lined shower enclosure is studded at regular intervals with pale circular tiles that reflect light from the overhead fitting.
Right Light wood panelling gives a small bathroom a sophisticated look, and a large, unframed mirror increases the sense of space.
Opposite, above right A combination of hardwood decking and white mosaic tiles provides safe, moisture-resistant surfaces around a sunken bath.
Opposite, below right Loose-laid beach pebbles interspersed with uplighters form a natural border for a timber boardwalk floor.

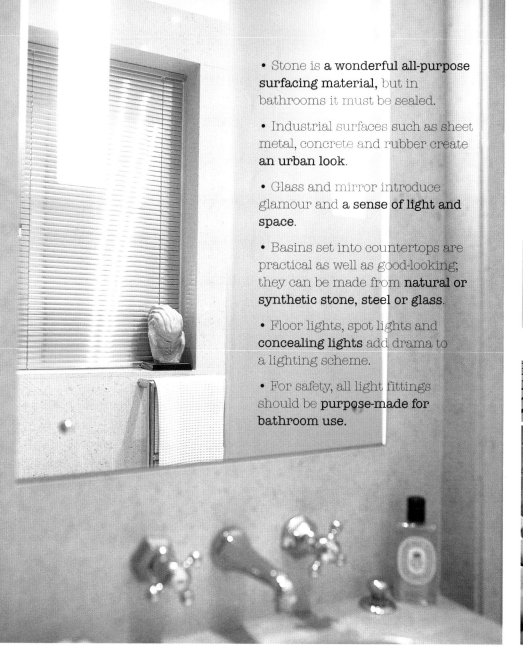

- Stone is **a wonderful all-purpose surfacing** material, but in bathrooms it must be sealed.

- Industrial surfaces such as sheet metal, concrete and rubber create **an urban look**.

- Glass and mirror introduce glamour and a **sense of light and space**.

- Basins set into countertops are practical as well as good-looking; they can be made from **natural or synthetic stone, steel or glass**.

- Floor lights, spot lights and **concealing lights** add drama to a lighting scheme.

- For safety, all light fittings should be **purpose-made for bathroom use.**

fixtures & appliances

There are fixtures to suit every kind of bathroom. To pick your way through the bathroom maze, first identify your priorities and your personal style. Make a wish-list of your ideal fittings, then whittle it down according to your budget, lifestyle and the space available. If you don't know what style you want, gather bathroom brochures, books and magazines and mark the pictures that appeal – you'll soon see if you lean towards modern or traditional shapes.

Above A mixer tap set into the marble top of a low partition wall at the foot of a bath projects into the tub to a lesser degree than it would do if it were wall- or rim-mounted, allowing for more comfortable bathing in a smaller than standard-size bathtub.

Right This custom-made glass basin – cantilevered from the wall with no visible means of support – is designed for washing under running water. Slim, shallow and with a backward-sloping base, it is long enough for two people to use at the same time, but it has a single plugless waste, so there is no possibility of water overflowing. Uncomplicated, wall-mounted taps add to the minimalist effect.

Above and top Countertop basins come in various shapes to suit the style of room and the available space. Taps to fill them should be wall-mounted or extra-tall deck fittings.
Left A traditional fixed shower rose provides no choice of invigorating spray patterns – simply a heavy, drenching rain of water, with separate crosshead handles to control temperature and flow.

Popular bathtub materials include cast iron, enamelled steel, pressed acrylic and cast synthetics. Cast iron is heavy and stable with a lustrous porcelain enamelled finish; enamelled steel is lighter, and pressed acrylic lighter still. Cast synthetics mimic cast iron but are lighter and warm to the touch.

Most built-in baths are rectangular and available in a range of standard sizes, but corner baths and tapered baths are an option in small or awkwardly shaped rooms. Freestanding baths made from cast iron or cast synthetics come in modern oval shapes as well as the traditional roll-top form. While antique-style tubs stand on decorative legs, the modern ones have chunky wooden legs and rest on the floor, or on wooden or stone stands. To make the bath the main feature in the room, consider bespoke tubs made from stone, wood or stainless steel or an antique tub in ceramic or copper.

In Europe as well as America, a shower is now regarded as an essential piece of bathroom equipment, in addition to or instead of a bathtub. A separate shower enclosure is the ideal, but if space is tight, an overbath shower is a practical

Above The sprays from these twin showerheads overlap to give an even coverage within the large, rectangular shower enclosure. The exposed pipework supplying them is so neatly stapled along the ceiling that it makes minimal impact on the decor.

Right Although the bathtub is similar in shape to a comfortable Victorian roll-top bath, instead of having decorative cast-iron legs, this contemporary copy rests on angular limestone cradles, giving it a cleaner, more streamlined look that is more appropriate in a modern bathroom.

alternative. Shower enclosures consist of a shower tray and a waterproof surround. Usually, the shower tray is made from steel or a rigid synthetic material. The surround can be simply an alcove tiled or faced with stone or some other waterproof material, an enclosure formed by two glass or acrylic panels or a self-contained shower cubicle. The door may be hinged, but, if space is restricted, choose bi-fold, sliding or pivoting doors that open without encroaching on the room.

The fittings that deliver the shower spray draw on stored hot water or heat the water as required. Showers that use stored

Top, left to right Supataps with the handle and spout made as a single unit have a retro charm. A shower head with tiny projections directs the water in fine jets to give an invigorating spray. A modern freestanding bath is filled from a simple chrome spout rising from the floor and curving smoothly over the rim.

Above, left to right The combination of a fixed wide shower rose and a hand-held shower allows a choice between a relaxing overhead drench or targeted showering. Separate controls for temperature and flow allow you to establish your ideal setting. A three-hole mixer tap has separate controls for hot and cold water.

water offer the greatest choice of fittings, including fixed-head and hand-held sprays. More powerful showers that incorporate body sprays, foot sprays and deluge sprays may need a pump to increase water pressure.

Washbasins are many and varied. The choice is between a pedestal basin which rests on a ceramic column that hides the pipework, a cantilevered wall-mounted basin, a vanity basin mounted under or integrated into a countertop, a console basin that rests on or is built into a decorative stand, and a countertop basin, rectangular, oval or round, which stands on a shelf or tabletop. Most basins are made from glazed ceramic but other materials such as glass, stone, cast synthetics, stainless steel and wood are becoming more widely available.

Lavatories and bidets are floor-standing or wall-mounted. Ceramic is the most prevalent material for these fixtures, although stainless steel is sometimes preferred for bathrooms with an industrial aesthetic.

Taps are available in a wide range of traditional, classic and contemporary designs to match the baths and basins they fill. Finishes include chrome, nickel, gold and various antique effects, and the most popular configurations are separate hot and cold pillar taps, three-hole mixers with handles to control hot and cold water and a separate spout and the monobloc or single-lever mixer tap, which controls the temperature and flow of the water.

Left The cistern and pipework for this wall-mounted bidet and lavatory are hidden in ducting, and the fixtures are suspended clear of the floor, so there are no awkward corners where dust and dirt can collect.
Below A valve-operated flush works efficiently and saves space but is not approved by every water authority.
Right This wide, shallow basin is a practical shape for washing and shaving.

- Before you buy a large bath made from **cast iron, stone or timber**, check that the floor will bear the combined weight of the tub and water.

- If you need extra storage, choose **a vanity basin with cupboard space below**. These can be made in contemporary or traditional styles.

- In a small bathroom, a shower cubicle with a sliding or folding door will open **without colliding with other fittings**.

- Unless you intend to use it simply for hand rinsing, buy the **largest bathroom basin** you can accommodate. It will contain splashes and allow for more **energetic washing**.

storage, furniture & accessories

A well-ordered bathroom is more conducive to relaxing, bathing and grooming than one that is littered with half-used shampoo bottles and damp towels. Good storage will bring the clutter under control. Built-in cupboards and vanity units generally provide bathroom storage, but there are situations where freestanding cabinets, rails, racks and containers are a useful addition or a practical alternative.

Left and above Glass shelves make efficient use of a space formerly occupied by a fireplace and its chimney. By day, the transparency of the shelves contributes to the room's open, airy atmosphere; at night, lights recessed into the top of the alcove beam through all the shelves, making a glowing display of the objects placed on them.

Opposite The bank of birchwood cabinets lining one side of this bathroom has twin washbasins mounted under its thick carrara marble countertop along with a series of cupboards and drawers. Raising the unit on short chrome legs makes the floor area seem larger and the unit itself less bulky.

Storage in a bathroom should combine open shelves or glazed cabinets for display and closed storage for those items you would prefer to hide. In bathrooms where space or budget is limited, the traditional bathroom cabinet mounted on the wall above the basin provides basic storage for essentials.

Floor-standing cabinets, trolleys and shelf units are a useful addition to most unfitted bathrooms. Cabinets are generally low and square, with a cupboard or drawers or a combination of the two. Storage trolleys are designed for manoeuvrability and may be fitted with brakes so that they can be parked wherever they are needed. These mobile units range in style from mesh or polished metal trolleys to contemporary wooden designs and rustic painted cupboards.

Freestanding shelf units are efficient space savers. Like cabinets, they come in many materials. Glass shelves must be made from special toughened glass and have polished edges; they are ideal for small spaces since they allow light to pass through. Painted shelves are practical and easy to refresh with a new coat of paint when they begin to look shabby. Wire mesh is well suited to shelves, but the mesh will not contain spilt liquids.

Although wooden shelves manufactured for bathroom use will be protected with a durable finish, furniture that was designed for other rooms may not be so resistant to damage by bathroom products. Even in the smallest bathroom, space can be found to hang wall

This page Built-in and close-fitting cupboards and drawers turn unused spaces into storage. Stained plywood drawers fill the space under a concrete vanity unit; silky, pale birch cupboards and drawers are recessed into the wall; while a huge wardrobe with imposing panelled oak doors slots neatly into an alcove.
Opposite Simple and relatively inexpensive ideas can solve specific storage problems. An antique shelf fitted high on the wall at the foot end of the tub holds fresh towels within easy reach of the person using the overbath shower. A wicker hamper stores towels and spare lavatory paper, and a purpose-made wall- or door-mounted rack keeps magazines tidy.

shelves. Ready-made units are simply screwed to the wall, but cut-to-size shelves will fit any available space.

Towel rails keep towels tidy and allow them to air after use. Unheated towel rails are made of wood, plastic or metal and can be wall-mounted or floor-standing. The wall-mounted types take the form of a ring or a single or double straight rail supported on brackets in a design to match other wall-mounted bathroom accessories. Rings for hand towels are placed beside a basin or bidet, but straight rails are large enough to hold a bath towel. Floor-standing rails usually have more than one rail and allow several towels to air at once.

Right Invaluable in a bathroom where shelf space is limited, this slim vertical rail, reaching from floor to ceiling, supports towel rails, tooth mug and a swing-arm magnifying mirror that is adjustable to various levels.

Below left Every shower enclosure needs somewhere to rest the soap or sponge; this minimal stainless-steel holder is in keeping with the urban style of its concrete and mosaic surroundings.

Below right An alcove, recessed into the wall at eye level and tiled with the same mosaic, is roomy enough to hold a selection of hair-care and shower preparations.

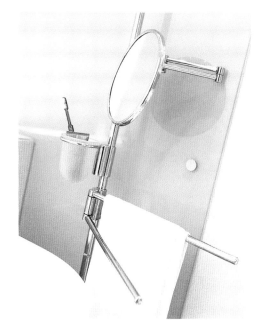

Individual wall-mounted holders for soaps, sponges, shaving equipment, toothbrushes and lavatory rolls can be fixed where they are needed. In the shower, corner-fitting shelves and tiered sets of wire baskets hold shower gel and shampoos within easy reach.

Most wall-mounted racks and holders are designed to be screwed to the wall, but in areas with tiled or glass walls, fittings that are attached by suction pads are easier to install.

Bath racks that rest like a bridge between the sides of the tub hold all the necessary equipment for bathing, and some luxurious models have an integral book rest, a candle holder or a shaving mirror.

Left Small, cylindrical pegs offer discreet hanging space for towels, bathrobes and toilet bags. The serpentine tubular heated towel rail has hinged fixings, allowing it to fold flat against the wall or swing out to hold thick towels or warm the room more quickly.
Far left Heated towel rails with wider spaces between groups of rails let air circulate freely, allowing towels to dry more quickly.
Below Laundry baskets do not have to be made of wicker – any moisture-resistant, washable material will do. If you choose a design such as this plywood bin that may also be used as a seat, check before you buy that it is sturdy enough for the purpose.

A laundry basket helps to keep the room tidy. Towels and clothes can be dropped into it the moment they are discarded. Some laundry bins are lined with a fabric bag which can be detached, allowing the laundry to be carried straight to the washing machine.

In most bathrooms, furnishings are limited to the essentials, but if you add a chair the atmosphere immediately becomes more relaxed and inviting. In a large, well-ventilated bathroom decorated in traditional or country style, an upholstered armchair brings comfort and a touch of luxury, but in a smaller space, light, moisture-resistant wicker or loom is a better choice. In a modern bathroom, a

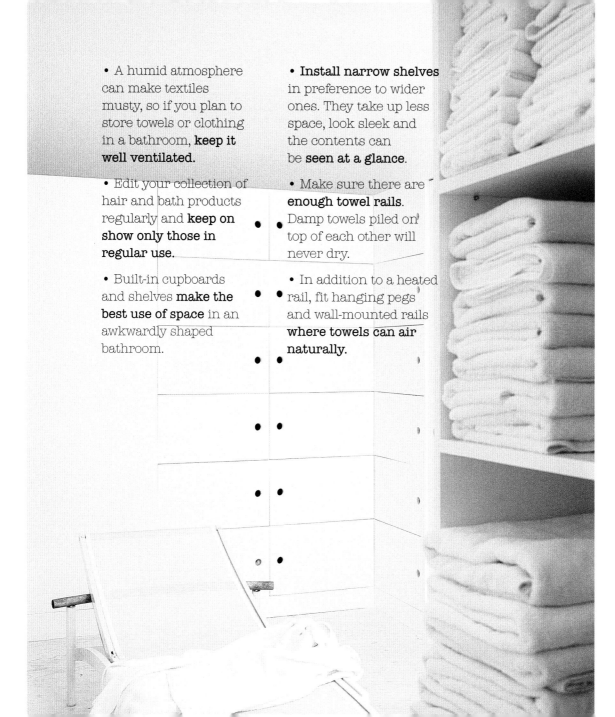

- A humid atmosphere can make textiles musty, so if you plan to store towels or clothing in a bathroom, **keep it well ventilated.**

- Edit your collection of hair and bath products regularly and **keep on show only those in regular use.**

- Built-in cupboards and shelves **make the best use of space** in an awkwardly shaped bathroom.

- **Install narrow shelves** in preference to wider ones. They take up less space, look sleek and the contents can be **seen at a glance.**

- Make sure there are **enough towel rails.** Damp towels piled on top of each other will never dry.

- In addition to a heated rail, fit hanging pegs and wall-mounted rails **where towels can air naturally.**

shapely plastic chair produced by one of the modern makers will be impervious to water and contribute to the contemporary style. Bathrooms too small for a chair generally have room for a stool or folding café chair.

The extra surfaces and storage provided by a small table, chest of drawers or small cupboard are not, strictly speaking, essential in a bathroom, but if you are aiming for a softer, more lived-in look than pared-down functionalism, they are a worthwhile addition.

A small table or cabinet drawn alongside the tub makes a suitable place to put your book, a drink and the radio while you indulge in a relaxing bath, and a chest of drawers with a mirror hung above it will serve as an attractive dressing table.

Above Magnifying mirrors are needed for tasks that require a close-up view; one that tilts and swivels is the most versatile.

Above left Wall-mounted shelves and holders are necessary adjuncts to a traditional pedestal basin that has limited space for essentials.

Left A bamboo stool is useful as a seat or surface and can withstand a moist atmosphere.

Far left The narrow shelf that runs the length of this bathroom is a valuable storage space; to avoid a cluttered effect, the items on it are arranged in neat groups.

Opposite Designed like a locker room, the walls of this bathroom/dressing room are lined with cupboards and open shelves.

bathrooms

styles

Right A semi-sunken bath screened by a low, toughened-glass panel barely impacts on the space in this small bathroom. Wall-mounted fittings let light flow uninterrupted around the room.

Below Unusually for a shower enclosure, the walls, rendered with the waterproof plaster used to line swimming pools, are slightly gritty to the touch, but the slate floor and reinforced-glass shelves offer a smooth contrast.

contemporary

The bathroom lends itself well to contemporary style. Its cool, smooth surfaces, sculptural fittings, and highly engineered plumbing combine to create a capsule environment of calm and order that is, for many of us, impossible to maintain with any success elsewhere in the home.

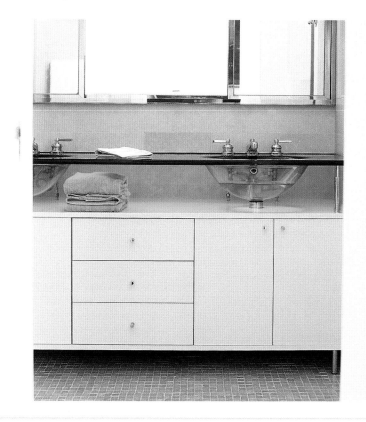

Above Hard surfacing need not mean a cold, spartan look. A large bath and even larger shower area lined with creamy limestone and frosted glass, lit to dramatic effect, create a warm and indulgent room.
Left Colour in a monochromatic scheme or a familiar material used in an unexpected way gives distinction to an essentially formal design. Here, the surprise element is the countertop. Made from blue glass with twin integral washbasins, the surface rises above a bank of plain, white cabinets, leaving a shelf between the two. Light passing through the glass illuminates the space beneath with an eerie glow.

The pioneers of the contemporary look in interior design were in search of simplicity to counter the complexity of modern life – and they turned to natural materials, naked and unadorned, to create it. A visually tranquil space undoubtedly has restorative powers, and although at first the materials and fittings needed to create it were expensive and readily available only to architects and designers, they have now come within reach of a wider public.

Surfaces that have the right aesthetic credentials for this look include natural materials such as hardwood and stone, and products such as brick, metal and concrete that have been used in the building industry for generations but were rarely visible in interiors. If you also take into consideration glass and modern artificial surfacing materials such as Corian and Lucite, the scope of contemporary style broadens to encompass a wide range of decorating options.

One of the most recent developments in contemporary bathrooms is the bolder use of colour. Previously, colour was limited to a natural palette based on the raw materials used for the decor, but gradually mosaic tiles – a cheaper surfacing

Left Metallic wallpapers inject light and drama into a dark bathroom; this one, depicting iconic film stars, adds a touch of glamour.
Above left Hanging a single vibrant picture can send shockwaves through the polite elegance of a dark monochromatic scheme.
Far left Many modern bathrooms incorporate natural materials, but those that include man-made surfaces are more colourful and vigorous. The colour in this shower room is at its most conspicuous in the transparent acrylic basin surround and shower screen.

material than stone or timber and available in shimmering, watery pastels that complement the natural tones – were added to give gentle contrast. More intense colours have followed in the form of synthetic surfaces and glass tiles, the latter being available in slip-resistant varieties for floors as well as walls.

Finding sanitary fittings, taps and showers in contemporary style has never been easier. The seminal designs of well-known architects and industrial designers will always be the purists' first choice, but the mass-market ranges they have inspired and the functional no-frills fittings made for the building trade make acceptable and affordable substitutes. Large, focal-point baths in stone, resin or timber; countertop basins in ceramic, glass, steel or stone; deceptively simple-looking taps; wall-mounted lavatories and bidets – all contribute to the modern look.

Above The design of some modern bathrooms has become formulaic, with the same materials and fittings appearing in different permutations. A uniquely personal effect that is no less stylish is achieved by combining disparate materials. This bathroom mixes wood veneer, aluminium, glass and ceramic tiles in an unusually muscular scheme.

Left Slate cut into thin tiles is suitable for both walls and floors, but because the stone is a dense, dark grey, rooms where it is used extensively must be brightly lit.

simplicity and clean lines . . .

If you need to partition the space in a bathroom, use **glass bricks or panels** – clear or frosted – to allow **light to flood through**.

Remember that **wood, stone and concrete** all need to be sealed to ensure that they are water-resistant.

Introduce colour in the form of mosaic, glass tiles or synthetic **surfacing materials**.

Sanitary fittings, taps and showers in **simple shapes** and wall-mounted lavatories with concealed cisterns all add to **the streamlined look**.

If you have the budget, a custom-made **countertop with an integral washbasin** is a sophisticated alternative to undermounted bowls.

for modern elegance

country

The dominant feature of a country-style bathroom is the bath. A vintage rolltop can take centre stage in a large room, while in a smaller space a standard tub placed along a wall and boxed in with panelling has a suitably nostalgic feel.

Above Antique fairs and sale rooms are the places to look for old bathroom fixtures such as this enamelled basin. Before you buy, check carefully for cracks and chips, which cannot be successfully repaired.

Right Painted wood panelling, a carpet on the floor and pictures on the wall give this bathroom a relaxed and homely air. The modern bath, raised on chunky turned wood feet and placed alongside a vintage washbasin, adapts well to its traditional surroundings.

Above Few modern basins are as pretty as this Victorian one with its floral transfer decoration. Modern reproductions are available, but they never accurately replicate the deep, inky, indigo blue that makes the original patterns unique.

Left The terrazzo floor, cast-iron bath and tiled walls have given good service for more than five decades. The decor still looks fresh and the addition of a pleated blind at the window and an industrial-style enamelled light fitting give it a cared-for look that does not detract from its retro charm.

Many bathrooms in traditional country homes have been converted from spare bedrooms, and frequently have enough space to allow a more imaginative layout than is possible in a contemporary bathroom. If they are retained, built-in cupboards, window seats, alcoves and other features of the original room add character. A smaller bathroom, built as an extension or squeezed into space partitioned from a large bedroom or landing, will need clever decoration to give it style.

Suitable reclaimed and reproduction fittings come in a variety of shapes, but if you are aiming to create a bathroom that is visually embedded in its surroundings, choose only those that match the status of the building. Victorian or Edwardian sanitaryware, perhaps

Left and far left Typical elements of country style include the stripped-pine door, traditional shower, fabric curtain and chunky wooden shelf.
Below Small details can have a big impact. These old enamel pots labelled 'soap' and 'sand' reinforce the traditional look.
Opposite, top Old and new come together in this vanity stand made by plumbing a modern basin into a painted antique chest.
Opposite, below left A sauna is part of everyday life in northern Europe, but still regarded as a luxury further south. As the temperature rises, the wood of the walls and benches fills the air with its resinous scent.
Opposite, below right A porcelain-handled spray distinguishes this traditional bath/shower mixer.

with floral decoration, is an appropriate choice for larger country houses, while in a modest country cottage simple fixtures in designs from the 1920s or 1930s would be more appropriate. Barns and other converted farm buildings are, by definition, modern, but fixtures in plain shapes are a good match for their pared-down character.

The bath is the dominant feature of a country bathroom. A rolltop model provides the right vintage look and has enough impact to stand in the centre of a large bathroom. In a smaller space, a standard bath placed along a wall and boxed in with tongue-and-groove panelling evokes a nostalgic feel.

Ceramic tiles and painted wood make excellent choices for wall and floor coverings in a traditional setting. Plain white or cream rectangular wall tiles hung brick-fashion have a retro look, but square tiles taken to eye level and edged with a narrow black border or a patchwork of patterned Victorian tiles would also work well. Tiles and timber are also ideal for flooring. For a more traditional result, create a chequered effect with black and white tiles or scrub the floorboards and leave them bare.

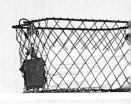

a new life for old things and . . .

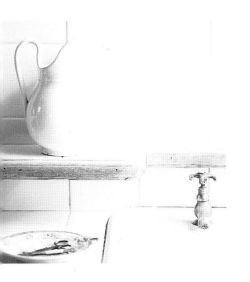

Choose fittings for **visual appeal**. A console washbasin with decorative **ceramic or metal legs** is an attractive alternative to an **urban vanity unit**.

Reproduction baths and basins take on **an authentic look** when fitted with antique taps.

Ceramic jugs, **enamel mugs** and other finds from bric-a-brac stalls make bathroom accessories with **the right period charm**.

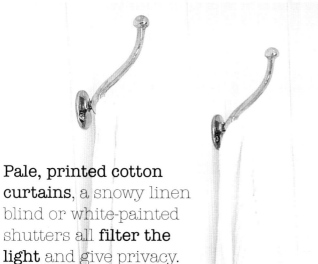

Pale, **printed cotton curtains**, a snowy linen blind or white-painted shutters all **filter the light** and give privacy.

If you need more storage, **search sale rooms or antique fairs** for cupboards or chests of drawers.

a breath of country air

Left and opposite The space to make an ensuite bathroom must sometimes be stolen from the bedroom itself. Less expensive than building a solid wall between the two zones, frosted-glass panels screening the washbasin and overbath shower areas give privacy where it is needed and contain the wet areas.

Below Building a shower under the roof slope in a loft conversion is effecive as long as there is full head height in the spot where the person using it will stand. However low the ceiling at the furthest point, a larger floor area will give a feeling of space within the enclosure.

compact

Lack of space is so common in a bathroom that it barely registers as a design challenge, but now that bathing is an act of self-indulgence as much as a daily routine, the room must reflect its dual role. A well-planned layout, careful use of colour and some ingenious design tricks will stretch the limits of a compact room, making it seem comfortable but never cramped.

A mixture of pale colours, clear glass and reflective surfaces can create an illusion of space in a compact bathroom. Moreover, improved plumbing and specially designed fixtures mean that there is no reason why smallness should preclude efficiency and elegance. The ensuite bathroom in a good hotel demonstrates how successful a small room can be. Rarely larger than is absolutely necessary, it contains all the essentials, yet still manages to convey a sense of luxury through its streamlined layout and use of top-quality fittings and surfaces. The domestic bathroom differs from this only in its need to include adequate storage.

In a compact space, cupboards and drawers are preferable to open shelves because they allow you to reduce the amount of clutter on view and make efficient use of otherwise dead areas under the basin, in alcoves and behind the panelling that conceals cisterns and pipework and encloses the bath.

The way fittings are arranged in a room influences how spacious it seems. As well as making a floor plan, it is worth drawing an elevation of each wall so you can take the height and bulk of the fixtures into account as well as the ground space they occupy. It is tempting to try to find room for all the fixtures on your wish list but sometimes the layout works better – and the room feels more open – if you compromise by having an overbath shower instead of a separate shower

Below Hinged doors require space to open, but in this shower room sliding doors have been fitted to the cabinets as well as to the entrance, allowing every little bit of floor space to be put to work.

Opposite, below Barely larger than an average cloakroom, this tiny shower room relies on good lighting and the pale colours of natural limestone to enhance its modest dimensions. A clear, frameless partition divides the space without visually compartmentalizing it.

Opposite, above Sometimes, because it is usually seen in the context of a larger room, a single imposing piece of furniture creates the illusion of space. Here, a large mirror, a glazed door and white walls balance the dark wooden vanity unit and ensure that it is not totally dominant.

enclosure or install a large shower instead of a tub. A less crowded room will feel relaxed, look better and be more convenient to use.

Visual devices to make a small room seem bigger include allowing light to flow through the space by choosing a frameless shower enclosure glazed with clear toughened glass – or even abandoning enclosures and partitions altogether in favour of a wet-room where all surfaces are waterproofed. Wall-mounted fittings make the floor area appear larger, and cabinets or vanity units that are raised on legs have a less bulky look. Even oddly shaped rooms can be made to feel more comfortable. For example, in a tall, narrow space, the perceived height can be reduced by tiling the walls to a level that stops short of the ceiling.

To reduce the apparent length of a long, narrow room, the tub can be placed across its width at one end, and an open shower area across it at the other. Arranging the other fixtures along one wall between them will give an impression of space at the centre of the room, which can be accentuated by putting mirrors on opposite sides of the room and hanging a lamp centrally over the area.

One way to give a more streamlined look both inside and outside a bathroom is to replace hinged doors with sliding pocket doors. Unlike track-mounted doors, which side over the wall they open onto, pocket doors are fitted in double-thickness walls and, when open, disappear into the space between the leaves of the wall.

light plays a crucial part . . .

Ducting may reduce the size of the room slightly but it **hides pipework** and the lavatory cistern, giving a neat look, and **storage can be recessed into it**.

Try **decorating the room** entirely in a single colour or material. **Continuity** adds to a calm, relaxed atmosphere.

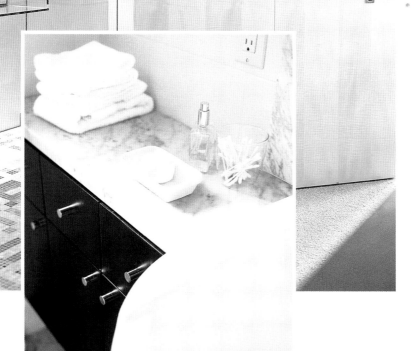

Cool, light colours such as **pale blue, lilac and aqua** seem to recede, making a room seem larger.

Make use of awkward spaces **in alcoves or under the eaves** for storage or activities that don't require **a full-height ceiling**.

in creating a sense of space

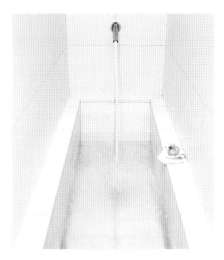

family-friendly

Families are never static, and in a household with young children the bathroom should be flexible enough to adapt as they grow. Get the basics right by providing efficient heating, waterproof surfaces and robust fittings that will stand up to the heavy wear they will inevitably receive, and respond to your children's developing tastes by changing the decor and accessories.

Above To prevent children locking themselves in the bathroom by accident, fit latches that can be opened from the outside.

Left An open-plan bathroom is a parents' sanctuary, but for children the opportunity to bathe in such a luxurious grown-up space is a special treat. A lockable door is essential if you want to keep this personal space private.

Right A few carefully selected accessories can alter the style of a plain white bathroom. A primary-coloured shower curtain and tooth mug will appeal to younger children and can easily be replaced as their tastes become more sophisticated.

Very young children need help with every aspect of personal care from teeth-cleaning to using the lavatory, so bathrooms designed for families must have plenty of clear space to allow parent and child to move around easily. The bath in particular needs enough space for a parent to kneel or sit beside the tub to supervise bathing, read stories or just discuss the day before helping their child towel dry and put on their pyjamas.

When choosing fittings, opt for a bigger bath – preferably with taps and plug hole placed centrally – so two children can bathe at the same time. If there is room, fit twin basins; they will be invaluable when children start school and the whole family needs to leave home at the same time in the morning.

Walls, floors and other surfaces should be both safe and practical. Floors must be waterproof, slip-resistant and warm to the touch. Materials such as rubber, linoleum, cork and vinyl have the right characteristics and, unlike ceramic tiles, provide a relatively soft landing if accidents do happen.

Left Built-in storage alcoves keep bathtime necessities close at hand.
Below A translucent plastic shower curtain with pockets doubles as an ever-changing display space for family photographs.
Opposite, left A square bath, which has been tailored to fit the space – with a ledge all around for toys and toiletries – is large enough to bathe two or three children at once.
Opposite, above right A wide shelf makes a useful changing area for a small baby, and open shelves offer easy-access storage.
Opposite, below right Twin basins save time in the morning rush hour, and mirrored cabinets recessed flush with the wall are less inviting to younger children.

Children tend to splash water around, and wall and surface materials that wipe down easily and won't be damaged by water are ideal. Tiles or special bathroom paints are the most tolerant wall treatments, while laminate, tile or stone surfaces for shelves and the tops of units are good-looking and robust.

Provide plenty of storage in the form of pegs to hold dressing gowns, laundry bags and towels, open shelves for things in frequent use such as toiletries, spare towels, baby-changing items and toys, and cupboards – some of them lockable – to keep potentially hazardous cleaning products, medicines and perfume sprays out of harm's way.

Try colour-coding toothbrushes, mugs and towels to remind children to use only their own personal kit and fit rails lower on the wall to encourage them to hang up towels. Allow early independence by providing sturdy, stable step stools to give easier access to the basin and lavatory.

thoughtful details help to make . . .

Make it **easy for children** to keep the bathroom tidy by fitting **pegs and rails** at a height they can easily reach.

To reduce the risk of falls choose **slip-resistant flooring,** mop up spilt liquids and keep the floor clear of toys, step-stools and **other obstacles**.

spaces fun for children

Choose a bright colour scheme. In case the decor outlasts your children's taste for **a primary palette**, introduce the colour in accessories and towels that can be **easily changed**.

Keep medicines and cleaners **under lock and key**.

Reduce the risk of scalding by opting for **a mixer instead of separate hot and cold taps**.

suppliers

FURNITURE & ACCESSORIES

The Chair Company
60 Eden Street
Kingston upon Thames
Surrey KT11 1EE
020 8547 2211
www.thechair.co.uk

Coexistence
288 Upper Street
London N1 2TZ
020 7354 8817
www.coexistence.co.uk

The Conran Shop
81 Fulham Road
London SW3 6RD
020 7589 7401
www.conran.com

Designers Guild
267–71 Kings Road
London SW3 5EN
020 7351 5775
www.designersguild.com

Geoffrey Drayton Interiors
85 Hampstead Road
London NW1 2PL
020 7387 5840
www.geoffrey-drayton.co.uk

George Sherlock
588 Kings Road
London SW6 2DX
020 7736 3955

Graham & Green
4 Elgin Crescent
London W11 2HX
020 7727 4594
www.graham
andgreen.co.uk

Habitat
0645 334433 for branches
www.habitat.net

Heal's
196 Tottenham Court Road
London W1P 9LD
020 7636 1666 or
0645 334433 for branches
www.heals.co.uk

The Holding Company
241–45 Kings Road
London SW3 5EL
020 7352 1600
020 8445 2888 for mail order
www.theholdingcompany.co.uk

Ikea
020 8208 5600 for branches
www.ikea.co.uk

Inhouse
28 Howe Street
Edinburgh EH3 6TG
0131 225 2888
www.inhouse.uk.com

John Lewis
278–306 Oxford Street
London W1A 1EX
020 7629 7111
www.johnlewis.co.uk
for branches

Ligne Roset
0845 602 0267 for stockists
www.ligneroset.co.uk

Marks & Spencer
173 Oxford Street
London W1D 2JR
020 7437 7722
020 7268 1234 for branches
www.marksandspencer.com

McCord
0870 907 0870 for mail order
www.emccord.com

Monsoon Home
020 7313 3000 for stockists
020 7313 4018 for mail order
www.monsoon.co.uk

Muji
020 7323 2208 for branches

Next
0116 286 6411 for branches
www.next.co.uk

Nicole Farhi Home
17 Clifford Street
London W1S 3RQ
020 494 9051

`Ocean
0870 2426283
www.ocean-furniture.co.uk

Ochre
22 Howie Street
London SW11 4AS
020 7223 8888
www.ochre.net

The Pier
01235 821088 for branches
www.pier.co.uk

Purves & Purves
220–24 Tottenham Court Road
London W1T 7QE
020 7580 8223
www.purves.co.uk

Selfridges
Oxford Street
London W1A 1AB
020 7629 1234
The Trafford Centre
Manchester M17 8DA
0161 629 1234
www.selfridges.com

Shaker
72–73 Marylebone High Street
London W1U 5JW
020 7935 9461

Skandium
72 Wigmore Street
London W1H 9DL
020 7935 2077
www.skandium.com

Sofa Workshop
01798 343400 for branches
www.sofaworkshop.com

Viaduct
1–10 Summers Street
London EC1R 5BD
020 7278 8456
www.viaduct.co.uk

Vitra
30 Clerkenwell Road
London EC1M 5PG
020 7608 6200
www.vitra.com

KITCHENS, WORK SURFACES & KITCHENWARE

Alternative Plans
9 Hester Road
London SW11 4AN
020 7228 6460
www.alternative-plans.co.uk

Bodum Home Store
24 Neal Street
London WC2 9PS
020 7240 9176
www.bodum.com

C. P. Hart
Newnham Terrace
Hercules Road
London SE1 7DR
020 7902 1000 for branches
www.cphart.co.uk

Divertimenti
33/34 Marylebone High Street
London W1U 4PT
020 7935 0689
and 139/141 Fulham Road
London SW3 6SD
020 7581 8065
www.divertimenti.co.uk

DuPont Corian
0800 962116
www.corian.com

Fired Earth
Twyford Mill
Oxford Road, Adderbury
Banbury
Oxfordshire OX17 3HP
01295 814300
www.firedearth.com

Fulham Kitchens
19 Carnwath Road
London SW6 3HR
020 7736 6458

Franke
0161 436 6280 for stockists
www.franke.co.uk

Ideal Standard and Sottini
The Bathroom Works
National Avenue
Hull HU5 4HS
01482 346461
www.ideal-standard.co.uk

Habitat
0645 334433 for branches
www.habitat.net

Johnny Grey
01730 821424
www.johnnygrey.co.uk

Kirkstone
01539 433296
www.kirkstone.com

Lakeland Limited
01539 488100
www.lakelandlimited.com
for mail order

John Lewis
Oxford Street
London W1A 1EX
020 7629 7711 ext. 4800
www.johnlewis.co.uk
for branches

Miele UK
01235 233533 for stockists
www.miele.co.uk

Plain English
The Tannery
Combs
Stowmarket
Suffolk IP14 2EN
01449 774028

Poggenpohl
0800 243781 for stockists
www.poggenpohl.de

Purves & Purves
220–24 Tottenham Court Road
London W1T 7QE
020 7580 8223
www.purves.co.uk

BEDS & BEDROOM FURNITURE

Amazing Emporium
249 Cricklewood Broadway
London NW2 6NX
020 8208 1616
www.amazingemporium.com

And So To Bed
Showrooms nationwide
0808 1444343 for stockists
www.andsotobed.co.uk

Beaudesert
Old Imperial Laundry
London SW11 4XW
020 7720 4977
www.beaudesert.co.uk

California Closets
Unit 8, Staples Corner
Business Park
London NW2 7JP
020 8208 4544
www.calclosets.co.uk

Cath Kidston
8 Clarendon Cross
London W11 4AP
020 7221 4000
(and stockists)
www.cathkidston.co.uk

The Conran Shop
Michelin House
81 Fulham Road
London SW3 6RD
020 7589 7401
www.conran.co.uk

Couverture
310 Kings Road
London SW3 5UH
020 7795 1200
www.couverture.co.uk

Designers Guild
267–71 Kings Road
London SW3 5EN
(and stockists)
020 7243 7300
www.designersguild.com

Habitat
196 Tottenham Court Road
London W1T 9LD
020 7631 3880
0845 6010740 for branches
www.habitat.net

Harriet Ann Sleigh Beds
Cherry Garden Farm
Hastings Road
Rolvenden, Cranbrook
Kent TN17 4PL
01580 243005 for stockists

Heal's
196 Tottenham Court Road
London W1T 7LQ
020 7636 1666
www.heals.co.uk

The Holding Company
241–45 Kings Road
London SW3 5EL
020 7352 1600
(and mail order)
www.theholdingcompany.co.uk

Ikea
0845 355 1141
www.ikea.co.uk

Feather & Black
83 Tottenham Court Road
London W1T 4SZ
020 7436 7707
01243 380600 for catalogue
www.featherandblack.com

Laura Ashley
0871 9835 999
www.lauraashley.com
for branches

The London Wall Bed Company
430 Chiswick High Road
London W4 5TF
020 8742 8200
www.wallbed.co.uk

Marks & Spencer
173 Oxford Street
London W1D 2JR
020 7437 7722
020 7268 1234 for branches
www.marksandspencer.com

Melin Tregwynt
Tregwynt Mill
Castlemorris
Haverfordwest
Pembrokeshire SA62 5UX
01348 891225
www.melintregwynt.co.uk

Ocean
0870 2426283
www.ocean-furniture.co.uk

Oka
0870 160 6002
www.okadirect.com

Peacock Blue
0870 333 1555
www.peacockblue.co.uk

R. J. Norris
88 Coldharbour Lane
London SE5 9PU
020 7274 5306
www.norrisbedding.co.uk

The White Company
0870 900 9555
www.thewhiteco.com

**BATHROOMS & BATHROOM
ACCESSORIES**

Aqualisa Products
The Flyers Way
Westerham
Kent TN16 1DE
01959 563240
www.aqualisa.co.uk

Armitage Shanks
Armitage
Rugeley
Staffordshire WS15 4BT
01543 490253
www.armitage-shanks.co.uk

Aston Matthews
141–47 Essex Road
London N1 2SN
020 7226 7220
www.astonmatthews.co.uk

Bathstore.com
410–14 Upper
Richmond Road
London SW14 7JX
020 8870 8888
(and stores nationwide)
www.bathstore.com

Bathroom City
Tyseley Industrial Estate
Birmingham B25 8ET
0121 753 0700
www.bathroomcity.co.uk

Colourwash
165 Chamberlayne Road
London NW10 3NU
020 8459 8918
www.colourwash.co.uk

C. P. Hart
Newnham Terrace
Hercules Road
London SE1 7DR
020 7902 1000 or
www.cphart.co.uk
for branches

Czech & Speake
39c Jermyn Street
London SW1Y 6DN
020 8980 4567
www.czechspeake.com

Fired Earth
Twyford Mill
Oxford Road, Adderbury
Banbury
Oxfordshire OX17 3HP
01295 814300
www.firedearth.com

Ideal Standard and Sottini
The Bathroom Works
National Avenue
Hull HU5 4HS
01482 499380

Majestic Shower Company
1 North Place
Edinburgh Way, Harlow
Essex CN20 2SL
01279 443644
www.majesticshowers.com

Marks & Spencer
173 Oxford Street
London W1D 2JR
020 7437 7722
020 7268 1234 for branches
www.marksandspencer.com

Mira
Cromwell Road
Cheltenham
Gloucestershire GL52 5EP
01242 221221
www.mirashowers.com

Nordic
Unit 5, Fairview Estate
Holland Road
Hurst Green, Oxted
Surrey RH8 9BZ
01882 716111
www.nordic.co.uk

Old Fashioned Bathrooms
The Foresters Hall
52 High Street
Debenham
Suffolk IP14 6QW
01728 860926
www.oldfashioned
bathrooms.co.uk

Samuel Heath & Sons
Leopold Street
Birmingham B12 0UJ
0800 0191 282
www.samuel-heath.com

Shires Bathrooms
Beckside Road
Bradford
West Yorkshire BD7 2JE
01274 521199
www.shires-bathrooms.co.uk

Triton
Newdagate Street
Nuneaton
Warwickshire CV11 4EU
01203 344441
www.tritonshowers.co.uk

Vernon Tutbury
Silverdale
Newcastle-under-Lyme
Staffordshire ST5 6EL
01782 717175
www.qpinteriors.co.uk

Villeroy & Boch
267 Merton Road
London SW18 5JS
020 8871 4028
www.villeroy-boch.com

Vola
Unit 12
Ampthill Business Park
Station Road, Ampthill
Bedfordshire MK45 2QW
01525 841155
www.vola.co.uk

Water Monopoly
16–18 Lonsdale Road
London NW6 6RD
020 7624 2636
www.watermonopoly.co.uk

LIGHTING

Aktiva
020 7428 9325
www.aktiva.co.uk

British Home Stores
129–37 Marylebone Road
London NW1 5QD
www.bhs.co.uk
for branches

Chelsea Lighting Design
Unit 1, 23A Smith Street
London SW3 4EJ
www.chelsealighting.co.uk

Christopher Wray Lighting
8–10 Headingley Lane
Leeds LS6 2AS
020 7751 8701 for branches
www.christopherwray.co.uk

Hector Finch Lighting
88–90 Wandsworth Bridge Road
London SW6 2TF
020 7731 8886

John Cullen Lighting
585 Kings Road
London SW6 2EH
020 7371 5400
www.johncullenlighting.co.uk

John Lewis
Oxford Street
London W1A 1EX
020 7629 7711
www.johnlewis.com
for branches

FLOORING

Altro Floors
01462 480480 for stockists
www.altro.co.uk

Amtico
024 7686 1500
www.amtico.com

Dalsouple
01984 667551 for stockists
www.dalsouple.com

Delabole Slate
01840 212242
www.delaboleslate.com

Fired Earth
Twyford Mill
Oxford Road, Adderbury
Banbury
Oxfordshire OX17 3HP
01295 814300
www.firedearth.com

Junckers
01376 517512 for stockists
www.junckers.co.uk

Marmoleum
01592 643777 for stockists
www.marmoleum.co.uk

Roger Oates Design
The Long Barn
Eastnor
Ledbury
Herefordshire HR8 1EL
01531 631611 for stockists
www.rogeroates.com

Wicanders
01403 710001 for stockists
www.amorim.com

PAINTS & WALLPAPERS

B&Q
0845 3093099 for branches
www.diy.com

Sanderson
01895 830044 for nationwide
stockists
www.sanderson-uk.com

picture credits

Endpapers ph Jan Baldwin/the Meiré family home, designed by Marc Meiré; **Page 1 ph** Polly Wreford/home of 27.12 Design Ltd., Chelsea, NYC; **2–3 main ph** Andrew Wood/Mikko Puotila's apartment in Espoo, Finland, interior design by Ulla Koskinen; **3 inset left ph** Andrew Wood/Phillip Low, New York; **3 inset centre ph** Alan Williams/Stanley & Nancy Grossman's apartment in New York designed by Jennifer Post Design; **3 inset right ph** Chris Everard/Fred Wadsworth's flat in London designed by Littman Goddard Hogarth; **4l ph** Debi Treloar/Julia & David O'Driscoll's house in London; **4c ph** Debi Treloar/new build house in Notting Hill designed by Seth Stein Architects; **4r ph** Debi Treloar/Sudi Pigott's house in London; **5 ph** Debi Treloar/Fifth Avenue Residence, New York City designed by Bruce Bierman Design, Inc.; **6 ph** Jan Baldwin/Interior Designer Didier Gomez's apartment in Paris; **7al & 7b ph** Chris Everard/a house in London designed by Helen Ellery of The Plot London; **7ar ph** Jan Baldwin; **7cl ph** Jan Baldwin/Jan Hashey and Yasuo Minagawa; **8–9 ph** Andrew Wood/David Jermyn's house in London, designed by Woolf Architects (020 7428 9500); **10 ph** Chris Everard/Mark Weinstein's apartment in New York designed by Lloyd Schwan; **10–11 ph** Chris Everard/an apartment in Milan designed by Tito Canella of Canella & Achilli Architects; **11 ph** Andrew Wood /Alastair Hendy & John Clinch's apartment in London designed by Alastair Hendy; **11** illustration by Russell Bell; **12–13 & 13al ph** Andrew Wood/Rosa Dean & Ed Baden-Powell's apartment in London, designed by Urban Salon (020 7357 8800); **13ar ph** Chris Everard/an apartment in Milan designed by Tito Canella of Canella & Achilli Architects; **13br ph** Chris Everard/Adèle Lakhdari's home in Milan; **14 ph** Jan Baldwin/Olivia Douglas & David DiDomenico's apartment in New York designed by CR Studio Architects, PC; **14–15 ph** Chris Everard/an apartment in Paris designed by architects Guillaume Terver and Fabienne Couvert of cxt sarl d'architecture; **15a ph** Chris Everard/Mark Weinstein's apartment in New York designed by Lloyd Schwan; **15b ph** Chris Everard/Yuen-Wei Chew's apartment in London designed by Paul Daly Design Studio Ltd; **16al ph** Tom Leighton/interior designer Philip Hooper's own house in East Sussex; **16cl ph** Alan Williams/the Arbuthnott family's house near Cirencester designed by Nicholas Arbuthnott, fabrics designed by Vanessa Arbuthnott; **16bc ph** Chris Everard/Hudson Street Loft designed by Moneo Brock Studio; **16br ph** Alan Williams/Lindsay Taylor's apartment in Glasgow; **17al ph** Chris Everard/Pemper and Rabiner home in New York designed by David Khouri of Comma; **17ar ph** Alan Williams/Selworthy apartment in London designed by Gordana Mandic & Peter Tyler at Buildburo (www.buildburo.co.uk); **17bl ph** Alan Williams/New York apartment designed by Bruce Bierman; **17br ph** Catherine Gratwicke/Jonathan Adler & Simon Doonan's apartment in New York; **18 ph** Catherine Gratwicke/Martin Barrell & Amanda Sellers' flat, owners of Maisonette, London; **18–19 ph** Alan Williams/director of design consultants Graven Images, Janice Kirkpatrick's apartment in Glasgow; **19 ph** Chris Everard/apartment in Antwerp designed by Claire Bataille & Paul ibens; **20l ph** Andrew Wood/the Kjaerholms' family home in Rungsted, Denmark; **20r ph** Jan Baldwin/Emma Wilson's house in London; **21 ph** Andrew Wood/Michael Asplund's apartment in Stockholm, Sweden; **22a ph** Polly Wreford/an apartment in New York designed by Belmont Freeman Architects; **22b ph** Chris Everard/interior designer Ann Boyd's own apartment in London; **23al ph** Jan Baldwin/Jan Hashey and Yasuo Minagawa; **23ac ph** Andrew Wood/Roger & Fay Oates' house in Ledbury; **23ar ph** Chris Everard/Eric De Queker's apartment in Antwerp; **23b ph** Andrew Wood/a house in Stockholm, Sweden; **24l ph** Catherine Gratwicke/Francesca Mills' house in London, cushions from After Noah; **24ar ph** Polly Wreford/Louise Jackson's house in London; **24br ph** Polly Wreford/Clare Nash's house in London; **25l ph** Jan Baldwin/Clare Mosley's house

in London; **25r ph** Catherine Gratwicke/Lulu Guinness's home in London; **26–27 ph** Andrew Wood/Chelsea loft apartment in New York designed by The Moderns; **27l ph** Caroline Arber/Rosanna Dickinson's home in London; **27r ph** James Merrell; **28a ph** Catherine Gratwicke/Sasha Gibb, colourist, interior consultant and designer; **28bl ph** James Merrell; **28bc ph** Polly Eltes/a house in London designed by Charlotte Crosland Interiors; **28br ph** Henry Bourne; **29 ph** James Merrell/an apartment in New York designed by James Biber of Pentagram with curtain design by Mary Bright; **30 & 31b ph** Andrew Wood/architecture and furniture by Spencer Fung Architects (020 8960 9883); **31al ph** Polly Wreford; **31ar ph** Andrew Wood; **32al ph** Catherine Gratwicke; **32ar ph** Chris Everard/David Mullman's apartment in New York designed by Mullman Seidman Architects; **32b ph** Jan Baldwin/Mona Nerenberg and Lisa Bynon's house in Sag Harbor; **33a ph** Jan Baldwin/interior architect Joseph Dirand's apartment in Paris; **33bl ph** Chris Everard/architect Jonathan Clark's home in London; **33r ph** Polly Wreford/Robert Merrett and Luis Peral's apartment in London; **34a ph** Chris Tubbs/Daniel Jasiak's home near Biarritz; **34bl ph** Henry Bourne; **34br ph** Andrew Wood; **35 ph** Catherine Gratwicke; **36–37 ph** Andrew Wood/Mikko Puotila's apartment in Espoo, Finland, interior design by Ulla Koskinen; **38 ph** Chris Everard/Jo Warman – Interior Concepts; **39 ph** Chris Everard/apartment in Antwerp designed by Claire Bataille & Paul ibens; **40l ph** Chris Everard/architect Jonathan Clark's home in London; **40r ph** Andrew Wood/Mikko Puotila's apartment in Espoo, Finland, interior design by Ulla Koskinen; **41al ph** Alan Williams /the architect Voon Wong's own apartment in London; **41ar ph** Chris Everard/an apartment in New York designed by Gabellini Associates; **41b ph** Chris Everard/an apartment in Milan designed by Tito Canella of Canella & Achilli Architects; **42a ph** Alan Williams/Alannah Weston's house in London designed by Stickland Coombe Architecture; **42b ph** Chris Everard/Ian Chee of VX design & architecture; **42–43a ph** Andrew Wood/a house in Stockholm, Sweden; **42–43b ph** Alan Williams/Stanley & Nancy Grossman's apartment in New York designed by Jennifer Post Design; **43ar ph** Andrew Wood/Christer Wallensteen's apartment in Stockholm, Sweden, lighting by Konkret Architects/Gerhard Rehm; **43b ph** Andrew Wood/Mikko Puotila's apartment in Espoo, Finland, interior design by Ulla Koskinen; **44 ph** Christopher Drake/designer Barbara Davis' own house in upstate New York; **44–45 ph** James Merrell; **45a & b ph** Chris Tubbs/Nickerson-Wakefield House in upstate New York/anderson architects; **46l ph** Christopher Drake/Nelly Guyot's house in Ramatuelle, France, styled by Nelly Guyot; **46a & br ph** Chris Tubbs/Jonathan Adler and Simon Doonan's house on Shelter Island near New York designed by Schefer Design; **47l ph** Chrstopher Drake/Ali Sharland's house in Gloucestershire; **47a & br ph** Catherine Gratwicke/designer Caroline Zoob's home in East Sussex, selection of cushions made from antique fabrics by Caroline Zoob; **48 all ph** Simon Upton; **49al ph** Henry Bourne; **49al & r ph** James Merrell; **49ar ph** Chris Tubbs/Clara Baillie's house on the Isle of Wight; **50al ph** Andrew Wood/Neil Bingham's house in Blackheath, London, chair courtesy of Designers Guild; **50bl ph** Tom Leighton; **50–51 ph** Andrew Wood/Century (020 7487 5100); **51 ph** Andrew Wood/Ian Chee of VX design & architecture, chair courtesy of Vitra; **52l ph** Andrew Wood; **52c ph** Chris Everard; **52–53 ph** Polly Wreford/an apartment in New York designed by Belmont Freeman Architects; **53bl ph** Andrew Wood/Phillip Low, New York; **53 main ph** Polly Wreford/home of 27.12 Design Ltd., Chelsea, NYC; **53r ph** Polly Wreford; **54l ph** Chris Everard/Adèle Lakhdari's home in Milan; **54–55 ph** Catherine Gratwicke/Laura Stoddart's apartment in London; **55 ph** Polly Wreford; **56al ph** Tom Leighton; **56bl ph** Chris Everard/François Muracciole's apartment in Paris; **56–57 ph** Polly Wreford/Ros Fairman's house in London; **57a ph** Andrew Wood/a house in London designed by Guy Stansfeld (020 7727 0133); **57bl ph** Catherine Gratwicke **57br ph** Catherine Gratwicke/Martin Barrell and Amanda Sellers' flat, owners of Maisonette, London; **58l ph** Debi Treloar/architect Simon Colebrook's home in London; **58–59 ph** Debi Treloar/Imogen Chappel's home in Suffolk; **59a ph** Debi Treloar; **59b ph** Debi Treloar/Eben & Nica Cooper's bedroom, the Cooper family playroom; **60l ph**

Debi Treloar; **60br ph** Debi Treloar/designed by Ash Sakula Architects; **60–61a ph** Debi Treloar/Catherine Chermayeff & Jonathan David's family home in New York designed by Asfour Guzy Architects; **61l ph** Debi Treloar/a family home in London, portraits by artist Julian Opie, Lisson Gallery; **61ar ph** Debi Treloar/ Elizabeth Alford and Michael Young's loft in New York; **61br ph** Debi Treloar/the Zwirners' loft in New York; **62–63 ph** Chris Everard/Nadav Kander & Nicole Verity's house; **64l ph** James Merrell/a house in Sydney designed by Luigi Rosselli; **64r ph** Andrew Wood/Nik Randall, Suzsi Corio and Louis' home in London designed by Brookes Stacey Randall; **64–65 ph** Chris Everard/Kampfner's house in London designed by Ash Sakula Architects; **65** illustration by Shonagh Rae; **66a ph** Andrew Wood/Nello Renault's loft in Paris; **66b ph** Chris Everard/Hudson Street Loft, designed by Moneo Brock Studio; **67l ph** Andrew Wood/Andrew Noble's apartment in London designed by Nico Rensch Architeam; **67r ph** Chris Everard/ designed by Mullman Seidman Architects; **68l ph** Andrew Wood/a house in London designed by Bowles and Linares; **68c ph** Chris Everard/Vicson Guevara's apartment in New York designed by Yves-Claude Design; **68r ph** Chris Everard/ David Mullman's apartment in New York designed by Mullman Seidman Architects; **69 ph** Chris Everard/the London apartment of the Sheppard Day Design Partnership; **70al ph** Chris Everard/Hudson Street Loft, designed by Moneo Brock Studio; **70ar ph** James Merrell/a house in Pennsylvania designed by Laura Bohn and built by Richard Fiore/BFI Construction; **70bl ph** Alan Williams/Margot Feldman's house in New York designed by Patricia Seidman of Mullman Seidman Architects; **70br ph** Alan Williams/Katie Bassford King's house in London designed by Touch Interior Design; **71l ph** Alan Williams/interior designer and Managing Director of the Société Yves Halard, Michelle Halard's own apartment in Paris; **71r ph** Andrew Wood/Alastair Hendy & John Clinch's apartment in London designed by Alastair Hendy; **72a ph** Chris Everard/Hudson Street Loft, designed by Moneo Brock Studio; **72bl ph** Andrew Wood/Ian Bartlett & Christine Walsh's house in London; **72br ph** Chris Everard/Vicson Guevara's apartment in New York designed by Yves-Claude Design; **73a ph** Catherine Gratwicke/Kimberley Watson's house in London; **73bl ph** Andrew Wood/Dawna & Jerry Walter's house in London; **73br ph** Chris Everard/florist and landscape designer Stephen Woodhams' home in London, designed by architect Taylor Hammond, kitchen by Camarque; **74 ph** Jan Baldwin/Emma Wilson's house in London; **75l ph** Chris Everard/an apartment in New York designed by Gabellini Associates; **75ar ph** Chris Everard/Michael Nathenson's house in London; **75br ph** Jan Baldwin/Constanze von Unruh's house in London; **76a ph** Chris Everard/designed by Filer & Cox, London; **76bl ph** Andrew Wood/Alastair Hendy & John Clinch's apartment in London designed by Alastair Hendy; **76br ph** James Merrell/Consuelo Zoelly's apartment in Paris; **77 ph** Chris Everard/an apartment in New York designed by Steven Learner; **78l ph** Chris Everard/a house in London designed by Helen Ellery of The Plot London; **78r ph** Alan Williams/the architect Voon Wong's own apartment in London; **79a ph** Jan Baldwin/Emma Wilson's house in London; **79bl ph** Chris Everard/Gentucca Bini's apartment in Milan; **79bcl ph** James Merrell/a house in Sydney designed by Luigi Rosselli; **79bcr ph** Chris Everard/Ian Chee of VX design & architecture; **79br ph** Chris Everard/Andrew Wilson's apartment in London designed by Azman Owens; **80l ph** Henry Bourne/DAD Associates; **80r ph** Henry Bourne/a house in London designed by Mark Guard Architects; **81a ph** Ray Main/a house in London designed by Ash Sakula Architects; **81cl ph** James Merrell/an apartment in London designed by Ash Sakula Architects; **81bl ph** Ray Main/light from Hector Finch; **81bc ph** Andrew Wood/Alastair Hendy & John Clinch's apartment in London designed by Alastair Hendy; **81br ph** Ray Main/Jonathan Reed's apartment in London, lighting designed by Sally Storey, Design Director of John Cullen Lighting; **82l ph** Ray Main/a loft in London designed by Circus Architects, light from Fulham Kitchens; **82c ph** James Merrell/Stephen Woodhams' house in London designed in conjunction with Mark Brook Design; **82r ph** Ray Main/a house in London designed by Seth Stein and Sarah Delaney; **83 ph** Ray Main; **84l ph** Chris Everard/John Barman's Park Avenue apartment; **84r ph** Andrew Wood/Andrew Noble's apartment in London designed by Nico Rensch Architeam; **58al ph** Henry Bourne; **85bl ph** Andrew Wood/Phillip Low, New York; **85ar ph** Jan Baldwin/Emma Wilson's house in London; **85br ph** James Merrell/Andrew Arnott and Karin Schack's house in Melbourne; **86a ph** Catherine Gratwicke/Martin Barrell & Amanda Sellers' flat, owners of Maisonette, London; **86bl ph** Christopher Drake/Melanie Thornton's house in Gloucestershire; **86bc ph** James Merrell/Felix Bonnier's apartment in Paris; **86br ph** Chris Everard/François Muracciole's apartment in Paris; **87b ph** James Merrell/Douglas and Dorothy Hamilton's apartment in New York; **87al ph** Chris Everard/Gentucca Bini's apartment in Milan; **87ar ph** Andrew Wood; **87b ph** James Merrell/Felix Bonnier's apartment in Paris; **88r ph** Chris Everard/Arlene Hirst's New York kitchen designed by Steven Sclaroff; **88–89 ph** Chris Everard/designed by Filer & Cox, London; **89l ph** Jan Baldwin/Constanze von Unruh's house in London; **89r ph** Chris Everard/ photographer Guy Hills' house in London designed by Joanna Rippon and Maria Speake of Retrouvius; **90–91 ph** Andrew Wood/Rosa Dean & Ed Baden-Powell's apartment in London, designed by Urban Salon; **92 ph** Jan Baldwin/David Gill's house in London; **92–93 both ph** Chris Everard/Vicson Guevara's apartment in New York designed by Yves-Claude Design; **94l ph** Chris Everard/an actor's London home designed by Site Specific; **94r ph** Ray Main/Kenneth Hirst's apartment in New York; **95l ph** Jan Baldwin/Christopher Leach's apartment in London; **95ar ph** Henry Bourne/Felix Bonnier's apartment in Paris; **95cr ph** Andrew Wood/ Chelsea loft apartment in New York, designed by The Moderns; **95br ph** Chris Everard/architect Jonathan Clark's home in London; **96a ph** Alan Williams/the architect Voon Wong's own apartment in London; **96bl ph** Andrew Wood/Gabriele Sanders' apartment in New York, chairs from Totem; **96br ph** Chris Everard/Ou Baholyodhin & Erez Yardeni's penthouse, Highpoint, London; **97l ph** Andrew Wood/ Robert Kimsey's apartment in London designed by Gavin Jackson; **97ar ph** Chris Everard/Ian Chee of VX design & architecture; **97br ph** Debi Treloar/new build house in Notting Hill designed by Seth Stein Architects; **98–99 ph** Alan Williams/ Andrew Wallace's house in London; **99ar ph** Chris Everard/a house in London designed by Helen Ellery of The Plot London; **99bl ph** Catherine Gratwicke/Lucy and Marc Salem's London home, freestanding 'retro' kitchen by Marc & Lucy Salem; **99br ph** Catherine Gratwicke/Rose Hammick's home in London–French enamelled tins from Grace & Favour, 1950s curtains from Alexandra Fairweather; **100a ph** Catherine Gratwicke/Rose Hammick's home in London–checked sofa cover & red toile cushion from Nicole Fabre, 1920s gold cushion from Kim Sully Antiques; **100b ph** Henry Bourne; **101l & c ph** Chris Tubbs/Mike and Deborah Geary's beach house in Dorset; **101r ph** Simon Upton; **102al ph** Tom Leighton; **102bl ph** Simon Upton; **102r ph** Jan Baldwin/Clare Mosley's house in London; **103al ph** Henry Bourne; **103bl** Simon Upton; **103br ph** Henry Bourne; **104l ph** Chris Everard/Suze Orman's apartment in New York designed by Patricia Seidman of Mullman Seidman Architects; **104–105 ph** Jan Baldwin/Peter & Nicole Dawes' apartment, designed by Mullman Seidman Architects; **105br ph** Chris Everard/ Peter and Nicole Dawes' apartment, designed by Mullman Seidman Architects; **106l ph** Chris Everard/an apartment in Paris, designed by architect Paul Collier; **106r ph** Chris Everard/John Kifner's apartment in New York, designed by Mullman Seidman Architects; **107l ph** Andrew Wood/an apartment in Bath designed by Briffa Phillips Architects; **107r ph** Chris Everard/a London apartment designed by architect Gavin Jackson; **108al & c ph** Chris Everard/Programmable House in London, designed by d-squared; **108ar ph** Chris Everard/an apartment in Milan designed by Tito Canella of Canella & Achilli Architects; **108bl ph** Chris Everard/ an apartment in Paris, designed by architect Paul Collier; **108–109 ph** Chris Everard/an apartment in Paris designed by architects Guillaume Terver and Fabienne Couvert of cxt sarl d'architecture; **109r ph** Chris Everard/Pemper and Rabiner home in New York, designed by David Khouri of Comma; **110l ph** Chris Everard/Kampfner's house in London designed by Ash Sakula Architects; **110–11 ph** Debi Treloar/an apartment in London by Malin Iovino Design; **111br ph** Debi Treloar/David & Macarena Wheldon's house in London designed by Fiona

McLean; **112 ph** Debi Treloar/Imogen Chappel's home in Suffolk; **113l ph** James Merrell; **113al ph** Chris Everard/a house in London designed by Helen Ellery of The Plot London; **113ar ph** Debi Treloar/Victoria Andreae's house in London; **113cl ph** Henry Bourne; **113cr ph** Andrew Wood/the London flat of Miles Johnson & Frank Ronan; **114al ph** Debi Treloar; **114c ph** Vanessa Davies; **114b ph** Henry Bourne; **114–15 ph** Debi Treloar/Paul Balland and Jane Wadham of jwflowers.com's family home in London; **115bl ph** Debi Treloar/Sophie Eadie's house in London; **115br ph** Debi Treloar/Imogen Chappel's home in Suffolk; **116–17 ph** Debi Treloar/family home, Bankside, London; **118l ph** Debi Treloar/Elizabeth Alford & Michael Young's loft in New York; **118c ph** Debi Treloar/Sarah Munro and Brian Ayling's home in London; **118–19 ph** Chris Everard/Bob & Maureen Macris's apartment on Fifth Avenue in New York designed by Sage Wimer Coombe Architects; **119r ph** Chris Everard/an apartment in London designed by Jo Hagan of Use Architects; **120 ph** Jan Baldwin/interior designer Didier Gomez's apartment in Paris; **121a ph** Debi Treloar/Ben Johns & Deb Waterman Johns' house in Georgetown; **121b ph** Chris Tubbs/Vermont Shack/Ross Anderson, anderson architects; **122 ph** Debi Treloar/Ian Hogarth's family home; **122–23 ph** Alan Williams/Richard Oyarzarbal's apartment in London designed by Urban Research Laboratory; **123r** Alan Williams/Selworthy apartment in London designed by Gordana Mandic & Peter Tyler at Buildburo (www.buildburo.co.uk); **124bl ph** Alan Williams/owner of Gloss, Pascale Bredillet's own apartment in London; **124ar ph** Alan Williams/Donata Sartorio's apartment in Milan; **124br ph** Andrew Wood/an apartment in London designed by Littman Goddard Hogarth; **125l ph** Jan Baldwin/a house in New York designed by Brendan Coburn and Joseph Smith from Coburn Architecture; **125r ph** Polly Wreford/Louise Jackson's house in London; **126l ph** Tom Leighton; **126ar ph** James Merrell/Janie Jackson, stylist/designer; **126br & 127 ph** Alan Williams/Katie Bassford King's house in London designed by Touch Interior Design; **128l ph** Chris Everard/Jo Warman – Interior Concepts; **128–29 ph** Jan Baldwin/Emma Wilson's house in London; **129 ph** Chris Everard/apartment in New York designed by Gabellini Associates; **130l ph** Andrew Wood/Johanne Riss' house in Brussels; **130ar ph** Catherine Gratwicke/Claudia Bryant's house in London–headboard designed by Claudia Bryant; **130–31b ph** Chris Everard/an apartment in New York designed by Steven Learner; **131a** both Tom Leighton; **131c ph** Jan Baldwin; **131b ph** Jan Baldwin/Peter & Nicole Dawes' apartment, designed by Mullman Seidman Architects; **132al ph** Andrew Wood/media executive's house in Los Angeles, architect: Stephen Slan, builder: Ken Duran, furnishings: Russell Simpson, original architect: Carl Maston c.1945; **132ar ph** Jan Baldwin/Emma Wilson's house in London; **132b ph** Debi Treloar; **133a ph** Simon Upton; **133b both ph** Chris Everard/François Muracciole's apartment in Paris; **134a & bl ph** Chris Everard/Mark Weinstein's apartment in New York designed by Lloyd Schwan; **134br ph** Debi Treloar/Sarah Munro and Brian Ayling's home in London; **135 ph** Debi Treloar/family home, Bankside, London; **136 ph** Ray Main/Robert Callender & Elizabeth Ogilvie's studio in Fife designed by John C Hope Architects; **137al ph** Jan Baldwin/Olivia Douglas & David DiDomenico's apartment in New York, designed by CR Studio Architects, PC; **137bl ph** Jan Baldwin/designer Chester Jones' house in London; **137r ph** Catherine Gratwicke/designer Caroline Zoob's home in East Sussex; **138al ph** Chris Everard/Central Park West Residence, New York City designed by Bruce Bierman Design, Inc.; **138ar & b ph** Tom Leighton; 139a ph Catherine Gratwicke; **139b ph** Tom Leighton; **140 ph** Chris Everard/apartment of Amy Harte Hossfeld and Martin Hossfeld; **141al ph** Ray Main/Jonathan Reed's apartment in London, light from William Yeoward; **141ar ph** Jan Baldwin/Gabriele Sanders' Long Island home; **141b ph** Chris Everard/Jo Warman – Interior Concepts; **142a & bl ph** Catherine Gratwicke/Laura Stoddart's apartment in London; **142r ph** Debi Treloar; **143 ph** Ray Main/a loft in London designed by Nico Rensch, light from SKK; **144–45 ph** Chris Everard/Mark Weinstein's apartment in New York designed by Lloyd Schwan; **146 ph** Chris Everard/an actor's London home designed by Site Specific; **146–47 ph** Andrew Wood/Roger and Suzy Black's apartment in London

designed by Johnson Naylor; **147r ph** Chris Everard/Eric De Queker's apartment in Antwerp; **148l ph** Debi Treloar/new build house in Notting Hill designed by Seth Stein Architects; **148r ph** Andrew Wood/Johanne Riss' house in Brussels; **149a both ph** Alan Williams/Alannah Weston's house in London designed by Stickland Coombe Architecture; **149b ph** Jan Baldwin/art dealer Gul Coskun's apartment in London; **150al ph** Jan Baldwin/designer Chester Jones' house in London; **150cl ph** Chris Everard/Jo Warman – Interior Concepts; **150bl ph** Andrew Wood/media executive's house in Los Angeles, architect: Stephen Slan, builder: Ken Duran, furnishings: Russell Simpson, original architect: Carl Maston c.1945; **150r ph** Alan Williams/the architect Voon Wong's own apartment in London; **151al ph** Jan Baldwin/Gabriele Sanders' Long Island home; **151bl ph** Chris Everard/the London apartment of the Sheppard Day Design Partnership; **151ar ph** Andrew Wood/Richard and Sue Hare's house in Idaho designed by Mark Pynn A.I.A. of McMillen Pynn Architecture L.L.P.; **152l ph** Chris Tubbs/Daniel Jasiak's home near Biarritz; **152r ph** Christopher Drake/Melanie Thornton's house in Gloucestershire; **153 ph** Tom Leighton; **154al ph** Catherine Gratwicke/Rose Hammick's home in London–French antique sheet awning form Kim Sully Antiques, patchwork quilt by Emily Medley, shawl and flip-flops cushion from Grace & Favour, bed from Litvinof & Fawcett; **154bl ph** Tom Leighton; **154r ph** Catherine Gratwicke; **155l ph** Chris Tubbs/Mike and Deborah Geary's beach house in Dorset; **155ar ph** Tom Leighton; **155br ph** Tom Leighton/Mr Hone's 17th-century hutt in Shropshire; **156al ph** Debi Treloar; **156bl ph** Catherine Gratwicke; **156r ph** Simon Upton; **157a ph** Chris Tubbs/Daniel Jasiak's home near Biarritz; **157bl ph** Jan Baldwin/Gabriele Sanders' Long Island home; **157br ph** Chris Tubbs/Vermont Shack/Ross Anderson, anderson architects; **158 ph** Chris Everard/the London apartment of the Sheppard Day Design Partnership; **158–59 ph** Alan Williams/Katie Bassford King's house in London designed by Touch Interior Design; **159 ph** Jan Baldwin/art dealer Gul Coskun's apartment in London; **160a both ph** Alan Williams/Miv Watts' house in Norfolk; **160b ph** Chris Everard/Lisa & Richard Frisch's apartment in New York designed by Patricia Seidman of Mullman Seidman Architects; **161al ph** Catherine Gratwicke/Martin Barrell & Amanda Sellers' flat, owners of Maisonette, London; **161ar ph** Tom Leighton; **161b ph** Alan Williams/Stanley & Nancy Grossman's apartment in New York designed by Jennifer Post Design; **162ar ph** Jan Baldwin/interior designer Didier Gomez's apartment in Paris; **162c ph** Chris Everard/an apartment in Paris, designed by architect Paul Collier; **162bl ph** Tom Leighton/Roger & Fay Oates' house in Herefordshire; **163l & ar ph** Andrew Wood/Johanne Riss' house in Brussels; **163br ph** Tom Leighton/Roger & Fay Oates' house in Herefordshire; **164l ph** Christopher Drake/Diane Bauer's house near Cotignac; **164r ph** Debi Treloar/an apartment in London by Malin Iovino Design; **165 ph** Debi Treloar/Kate and Dominic Ash's home in London; **166–67 ph** Debi Treloar/Cristine Tholstrup Hermansen and Helge Drenck's house in Copenhagen; **168b ph** Debi Treloar/Kristiina Ratia and Jeff Gocke's family home in Norwalk, Connecticut; **168a ph** Debi Treloar/Sudi Pigott's house in London; **169a ph** Debi Treloar/Victoria Andreae's house in London; **169b ph** Debi Treloar/Kate and Dominic Ash's home in London; **170al ph** Debi Treloar/Suzanne & Christopher Sharp's house in London; **170bl ph** Debi Treloar/the Boyes' home in London designed by Circus Architects; **170ar ph** Debi Treloar; **170br ph** Debi Treloar/Sarah Munro and Brian Ayling's home in London; **171l ph** Debi Treloar/Wim and Josephine's apartment in Amsterdam; **171ar ph** Christopher Drake/Marisa Cavalli's home in Milan; **171br ph** Debi Treloar/Catherine Chermayeff & Jonathan David's family home in New York, designed by Asfour Guzy Architects; **172–73 ph** Henry Bourne/Dan and Claire Thorne's town house in Dorset designed by Sarah Featherstone; **174 both ph** Chris Everard/Fred Wadsworth's flat in London designed by Littman Goddard Hogarth; **175l ph** Chris Everard/an apartment in Paris designed by Bruno Tanquerel; **175r ph** Chris Everard /Simon Brignall & Christina Rosetti's loft apartment in London designed by David Mikhail Architects; **176l ph** Chris Everard/a house in London designed by Carden & Cunietti; **176r ph** Chris Everard/Andrew Wilson's house in London designed by Azman Owens; **177 ph**

Chris Everard/both Vicente Wolf's home on Long Island; **178l ph** Chris Everard/ Monique Witt and Steven Rosenblum's apartment in New York, designed by Mullman Seidman Architects; **178–79 & 179c ph** Andrew Wood /a house near Antwerp designed by Claire Bataille and Paul ibens; **179r ph** Chris Everard/Heidi Wish & Philip Wish's apartment in London designed by Moutarde & Heidi Wish; **180al ph** Ray Main/Client's residence, East Hampton, New York, designed by ZG DESIGN; **180ar ph** Chris Everard/a house in London designed by Carden & Cunietti; **180bl ph** Chris Everard/Andrew Wilson's apartment in London designed by Azman Owens; **180br ph** Chris Everard/New York City apartment designed by Marino + Giolito; **181l ph** Andrew Wood/Roger Oates and Fay Morgan's house in Eastnor; **181r ph** Alan Williams/Richard Oyarzabal's apartment in London designed by Urban Research Laboratory; **182l ph** Chris Everard/John Minshaw's house in London designed by John Minshaw; **182r** Henry Bourne/Linda Trahair's house in Bath; **183l ph** Chris Everard/Stephan Schulte's loft apartment in London; **183c ph** Andrew Wood/Roger and Suzy Black's apartment in London designed by Johnson Naylor; **183r ph** Andrew Wood/house in London designed by Bowles and Linares; **184l ph** Chris Everard/an apartment in New York designed by David Deutsch & Sidnam Petrone Gartner Architects; **184r ph** Chris Everard/designed by Zynk Design Consultants, One New Inn Square, a private dining room and home of chef David Vanderhook, all enquiries 020 7729 3645; **185l ph** Ray Main/ Jonathan Reed's apartment in London, lighting designed by Sally Storey, design director of John Cullen Lighting; **185ar ph** Chris Everard/Michael Nathenson's house in London; **185br ph** Chris Everard/Simon Brignall & Christina Rosetti's loft apartment in London designed by David Mikhail Architects; **186l ph** Jan Baldwin/ Peter & Nicole Dawes' apartment, designed by Mullman Seidman Architects; **186r ph** Chris Everard/a house in Hampstead, London designed by Orefelt Associates; **187l ph** Chris Everard/an apartment in Paris designed by Bruno Tanquerel; **187r ph** Jan Baldwin/Constanze von Unruh's house in London; **187br ph** Chris Everard/ architect Nigel Smith's apartment in London; **188a** Chris Everard/Richard Hopkin's apartment in London designed by HM2; **188b ph** Jan Baldwin/art dealer Gul Coskun's apartment in London; **189al & bc** Chris Everard/Heidi Wish & Philip Wish's apartment in London designed by Moutarde & Heidi Wish; **189ac** Chris Everard/Hudson Street Loft designed by Moneo Brock Studio; **189ar** Chris Everard/Freddie Daniells' apartment in London designed by Brookes Stacey Randall; **189bl** Chris Everard/Suze Orman's apartment in New York designed by Patricia Seidman of Mullman Seidman Architects; **189br ph** Jan Baldwin/ Christopher Leach's apartment in London; **190a ph** Chris Everard/Richard Hopkin's apartment in London designed by HM2; **190b ph** Chris Everard/New York City apartment designed by Marino + Giolito; **191 ph** Chris Everard/Pemper and Rabiner home in New York, designed by David Khouri of Comma; **192 ph** Chris Everard/designed by Mullman Seidman Architects; **193 both ph** Alan Williams/Gail & Barry Stephens' house in London; **194a ph** Chris Everard/Monique Witt and Steven Rosenblum's apartment in New York, designed by Mullman Seidman Architects; **194bl ph** Chris Everard/Heidi Wish & Philip Wish's apartment in London designed by Moutarde & Heidi Wish; **194br ph** Chris Everard/Michael Nathenson's house in London; **195al ph** Chris Everard/a house in Paris designed by Bruno Tanquerel; **195ar ph** Chris Everard/Suze Orman's apartment in New York designed by Patricia Seidman of Mullman Seidman Architects; **195b ph** Chris Everard/Mark Kirkley & Harumi Kaijima's house in Sussex; **196a ph** Chris Everard/ Alison Thompson & Billy Paulett's house in London designed by Stephen Turvil Architects; **196bl ph** Chris Everard/a house in London by Seth Stein; **196br ph** Debi Treloar/Ian Hogarth's family home; **196–97a ph** Chris Everard/Richard Oyarzabal's apartment in London designed by Jeff Kirby of Urban Research Laboratory; **197a ph** Chris Everard/a house in Hampstead, London designed by Orefelt Associates; **197b ph** Chris Everard/Freddie Daniells' apartment in London designed by Brookes Stacey Randall; **198 ph** Andrew Wood/Johanne Riss' house in Brussels; **199al ph** Chris Everard/New York City apartment designed by Marino + Giolito; **199ar ph** Chris Everard/Vicente Wolf's home on Long Island; **199bl ph**

Chris Everard/Simon Brignall & Christina Rosetti's loft apartment in London designed by David Mikhail Architects; **199br ph** Chris Everard/Paul Brazier & Diane Lever's house in London designed by Carden & Cunietti; **200–201 ph** Chris Everard/Calvin Tsao & Zack McKown's apartment in New York designed by Tsao & McKown; **202l ph** Chris Everard/Stephan Schulte's loft apartment in London; **202r ph** Chris Everard/ Ian Chee of VX design & architecture; **203l ph** Chris Everard/Monique Witt and Steven Rosenblum's apartment in New York, designed by Mullman Seidman Architects; **203r ph** Chris Everard/Freddie Daniells' apartment in London designed by Brookes Stacey Randall; **204a ph** Chris Everard/John Barman's Park Avenue Apartment; **204bl ph** Alan Williams/Hudson Street Loft designed by Moneo Brock Studio; **204br ph** Chris Everard/Sera Hersham-Loftus' house in London; **205l ph** Chris Everard/ Gomez/Murphy Loft, Hoxton, London designed by Urban Salon; **205r ph** Chris Everard/designed by Zynk Design Consultants, One New Inn Square, a private dining room and home of chef David Vanderhook, all enquiries 020 7729 3645; **206al ph** Chris Everard/a house in Hampstead, London designed by Orefelt Associates; **206bl ph** Debi Treloar/family home, Bankside, London; **206r ph** Debi Treloar/a house by Knott Architects in London; **207l ph** Andrew Wood/Johanne Riss' house in Brussels; **207c ph** James Morris/the Jackee' and Elgin Charles House in California's Hollywood Hills, designed by William R. Hefner AIA, interior design by Sandy Davidson Design; **207r ph** Chris Everard/Hilton McConnico's house near Paris; **208l ph** Tom Leighton/ lofts in the old centre of Amsterdam of Annette Brederode, painter & dealer & collector of antiques & 'brocante' and Aleid Röntgen-Brederode, landscape architect; **208r ph** Tom Leighton; **209l ph** Tom Leighton/Roxanne Beis' home in Paris; **209r** Sera Hersham-Loftus' house in London; **210bl ph** Chris Everard/a house in Hampstead, London designed by Orefelt Associates; **210ar ph** Chris Everard/Frazer Cunningham's house in London; **210br ph** Chris Everard/a house in Paris designed by Bruno Tanquerel; **211a both ph** Chris Everard/a house in London designed by Helen Ellery of The Plot London; **211b ph** Tom Leighton; **212al ph** Chris Everard/a house in Paris designed by Bruno Tanquerel; **212bl ph** Tom Leighton; **212r, 213l & 213ar ph** Debi Treloar/Kristiina Ratia and Jeff Gocke's family home in Norwalk, Connecticut; **213br ph** Chris Everard/Emma & Neil's house in London, walls painted by Garth Carter; **214 & 214–15 ph** Chris Everard/Alison Thompson & Billy Paulett's house in London designed by Stephen Turvil Architects; **215b ph** Jan Baldwin/a house in New York designed by Brendan Coburn and Joseph Smith from Coburn Architecture; **216l ph** Chris Everard/a house in Hampstead, London designed by Orefelt Associates; **216r ph** Chris Everard/an apartment in New York, designed by Mullman Seidman Architects; **217 ph** Chris Everard/Pemper and Rabiner home in New York, designed by David Khouri of Comma; **218 main ph** Chris Everard/Central Park West Residence, New York City designed by Bruce Bierman Design; **218 inset ph** Chris Everard/an apartment in New York, designed by Mullman Seidman Architects; **218–19 ph** Chris Everard/Fifth Avenue Residence, New York City designed by Bruce Bierman Design; **219bl ph** Chris Everard/Yuen-Wei Chew's apartment in London designed by Paul Daly Design Studio; **219ar & br ph** Chris Everard/Ben Atfield's house in London; **220l ph** Debi Treloar/Paul Balland and Jane Wadham of jwflowers.com's family home in London; **220r ph** Chris Everard/Monique Witt and Steven Rosenblum's apartment in New York, designed by Mullman Seidman Architects; **221 ph** Debi Treloar/Victoria Andreae's house in London; **222l ph** Debi Treloar/a house by Knott Architects in London; **222ar ph** Debi Treloar/Vincent & Frieda Plasschaert's house in Brugge, Belgium; **222br ph** Debi Treloar/Catherine Chermayeff & Jonathan David's family home in New York, designed by Asfour Guzy Architects; **223a ph** Debi Treloar/family home, Bankside, London; **223b ph** Debi Treloar; **224al ph** Debi Treloar/a family home in Manhattan, designed by architect Amanda Martocchio and Gustavo Martinez Design; **224bl ph** Debi Treloar/The Swedish Chair – Lena Renkel Eriksson; **224r ph** Chris Everard/Richard Hopkin's apartment in London designed by HM2; **224–25 ph** Debi Treloar; **225ar ph** Debi Treloar /Catherine Chermayeff & Jonathan David's family home in New York designed by Asfour Guzy Architects; **225br ph** Chris Everard/Simon Crookall's apartment in London designed by Urban Salon.

business credits

27.12 Design
+ 1 212 727 8169
www.2712design.com
Pages 1, 53 main.

Alastair Hendy
fax 020 7739 6040
*Pages 11, 71r, 76bl,
81bc.*

Alex Fairweather
07929 359425
Page 99br.

**Amanda Martocchio,
Architect**
189 Brushy Ridge Road
New Canaan, CT 06840
USA
Page 224al.

anderson architects
+ 1 212 620 0996
www.andersonarch.com
*Pages 45a, 45b, 121b,
157br.*

Ann Boyd Design
020 7351 4098
Page 22b.

**Annette Brederode and
Aleid Röntgen-Brederode**
Lijnbaansgracht 56d
1015 gs Amsterdam
Page 208l.

Asfour Guzy Architects
+ 1 212 334 9350
www.asfourguzy.com
*Pages 60–61a, 171br,
222br, 225r.*

Ash Sakula Architects
020 7837 9735
www.ashsak.com
*Pages 60br, 64–65, 81a,
81cl, 110l.*

Azman Owens Architects
020 7739 8191
www.azmanowens.com
Pages 79br, 176r, 180bl.

Asplund (showroom and shop)
+ 46 8 662 52 84
Page 21.

Barbara Davis
+ 1 607 264 3673
Page 44.

**Belmont Freeman
Architects**
+ 1 212 382 3311
Pages 22a, 52–53.

Bowles & Linares
020 7229 9886
Page 68l, 183r.

Brian Ayling, Artist
020 8802 9853
*Pages 118c, 134br,
170br.*

Briffa Phillips
01727 840567
Page 107l.

Brookes Stacey Randall
020 7403 0707
www.bsr-architects.com
*Pages 64r, 189ar, 197b,
203r.*

Bruce Bierman Design
+ 1 212 243 1935
www.biermandesign.com
*Pages 5, 17bl, 138al,
218 main, 218–19.*

Bruno Tanquerel
+ 33 1 43 57 03 93
*Pages 175l, 187l, 195al,
210br, 212al.*

buildburo
020 7352 1092
www.buildburo.co.uk
Pages 17ar, 123r.

Canella & Achilli Architects
+ 39 0 24 69 52 22
www.canella-achilli.com
*Pages 10–11, 13ar, 41b,
108ar.*

Carden Cunietti
020 7229 8559
www.carden-cunietti.com
Pages 176l, 180ar, 199br.

Caroline Zoob
(shop and mail order)
01273 476464
www.carolinezoob.com
Pages 47a&br, 137r.

Charlotte Crosland Interiors
020 8960 9442
www.charlottecrosland.com
Page 28bc.

Chester Jones
020 7498 2717
chester.jones@virgin.net
Pages 137bl, 150al.

**Christopher Leach
Design**
07765 255566
mail@christopherleach.com
Pages 95l, 189br.

Circus Architects
020 7953 7322
www.circus-architects.com
Pages 82l, 170bl.

Claire Bataille & Paul ibens
+ 32 3 231 3593
bataille.ibens@
planetinternet.be
*Pages 19, 39, 178–179,
179c.*

Clare Mosley
020 7708 3123
Pages 25l, 102r.

Clare Nash
020 8742 9991
Page 24br.

**Clark Johnson
Lighting Consultant**
Johnson Schwinghammer
+ 1 212 643 1552
*Pages 17al, 109r, 191,
217.*

Claudia Bryant
020 7602 2852
Page 130ar.

Coburn Architecture
+ 1 718 624 1700
www.coburnarch.com
Pages 125l, 215b.

Comma/David Khouri
+ 1 212 420 7866
www.comma-nyc.com
*Pages 17al, 109r, 191,
217.*

Coskun Fine Art London
020 7581 9056
www.coskunfineart.com
Pages 149b, 159, 188b.

Constanze von Unruh
020 8948 5533
www.constanzeinteriorpr
ojects.com
Pages 75br, 89l, 187ar.

Consuelo Zoelly
+ 33 42 62 19 95
Page 76br.

CR Studio Architects, PC
+ 1 212 989 8187
www.crstudio.com
Pages 14, 137al.

**cxt sarl d'architecture
Fabienne Couvert &
Guillaume Terver**
+ 33 1 55 34 98 50
www.couverterver-
architectes.com
Pages 14–15, 108–109.

d-squared design
020 7253 2240
www.d2-design.co.uk
Pages 108al, 108c.

DAD Associates
020 7336 6488
Page 80l.

Daniel Jasiak
+ 33 1 45 49 13 56
Pages 34a, 152l, 157a.

David Mikhail Architects
020 7377 8424
www.davidmikhail.com
*Pages 175r, 185br,
199bl.*

David Vanderhook
020 7729 3645
Pages 184r, 205r.

Dirand Joseph Architecture
+ 33 01 47 97 78 57
joseph.dirand@wanadoo.fr
Page 33a.

Dive Architects
020 7407 0955
www.divearchitects.com
*Pages 116–17, 135,
206bl, 223a.*

Dominic Ash Ltd
020 7689 0676
www.dominicash.co.uk
Pages 165, 169b.

Elizabeth Alford Design
+ 1 212 385 2185
esa799@banet.net
Pages 61ar, 118l.

Emily Medley
emilymedley@mac.com
Page 154al.

Emma Wilson
www.45crossleyst.com
*Pages 20r, 74, 79a,
85ar, 128–29, 132ar.*

Eric De Queker
DQ – Design In Motion
Koninklijkelaan 44
2600 Bercham, Belgium
Pages 23ar, 147r.

Felix Bonnier
+ 33 1 42 26 09 83
Pages 86bc, 87b, 95ar.

Filer & Cox
020 7357 7574
www.filerandcox.com
Pages 76a, 88–89.

Fiona McLean
McLean Quinlan
Architects
020 8767 1633
Page 111br.

Francesca Mills
020 7733 9193
Page 24l.

François Muracciole
+ 33 1 43 71 33 03
francois.muracciole@
libertysurf.fr
*Pages 56bl, 86br, 133b
both.*

Gabellini Associates
+ 1 212 388 1700
www.gabelliniassociates.
com
Pages 41ar, 75l, 129.

Garth Carter
Specialist interiors painter
07958 412953
Page 213br.

Gavin Jackson Architects
07050 097561
Pages 97l, 107r.

Gloss Ltd
020 8960 4146
pascale@glossltd.u-
net.com
Page 124bl.

Grace & Favour
35 North Cross Rd
East Dulwich
London SE22 9ET
Page 99br, 154al.

**Guard Tillman Pollock/
Mark Guard Architects**
020 7380 1199
www.markguard.com
Page 80r.

Guy Hills
Photographer
020 7916 2610
guyhills@hotmail.com
Page 89r.

Gustavo Martinez Design
+ 1 212 686 3102
gmdecor@aol.com
Page 224al.

Heidi Wish
020 7737 7797
*Pages 179r, 189a,
189bc, 194bl.*

Helen Ellery
The Plot London
020 7251 8116
www.theplotlondon.com
*Pages 7al, 7b, 78l, 99ar,
113al, 211a both.*

Hilton McConnico
+ 33 1 43 62 53 16
hmc@club-internet.fr
Page 207r.

Hirst Pacific Ltd
+ 1 212 625 3670
www.hirstpacific.com
Pages 94r.

HM2
020 7600 5151
andrew.hanson@harper-
mackay.co.uk
Pages 188a, 190a, 224r.

Hogarth Architects
(formerly Littman Goddard
Hogarth Architects)
020 7565 8366
www.hogartharchitects.
co.uk
*Pages 3 inset right, 122,
124br, 174 both, 196br.*

Imogen Chappel
07803 156081
*Pages 58–59, 112,
115br.*

Interior Concepts
020 8508 9952
www.jointerior
concepts.co.uk
*Pages 38, 128l, 141b,
150cl.*

Jackson's
020 7792 8336
Pages 24ar, 125r.

**James Biber, AIA/
Pentagram Architecture**
www.pentagram.com
Page 29.

Janie Jackson/Palma Lilac
020 8960 9239
Page 126ar.

Jennifer Post Design
+ 1 212 734 7994
jpostdesign@aol.com
*Pages 3 inset centre,
42–43b, 161b.*

Joanne Barwick
P.O. Box 982
Boca Grande
Florida 33921
USA
Page 156l.

Johanne Riss
+ 32 2 513 0900
www.johanneriss.com
*Pages 130l, 148r, 163l,
163ar, 198, 207l.*

John Barman Inc.
+ 1 212 838 9443
www.johnbarman.com
Pages 204a, 84l

John C Hope Architects
0131 315 2215
Page 136.

John Minshaw Designs
020 7258 5777
www. johnminshaw
designs.com
Page 182l.

Johnson Naylor
020 7490 8885
www.johnsonnaylor.com
Pages 183c, 146–47.

Jonathan Adler
+ 1 212 941 8950
www.jonathanadler.com
Pages 17br, 46a, 46br.

Jonathan Clark Architects
020 7286 5676
www.jonathanclark
architects.co.uk
Pages 33bl, 40l, 95br.

Josephine Macrander
+ 31 299 402804
Page 174l.

jwflowers.com
020 7735 7771
www.jwflowers.com
Pages 114–15, 220l.

Kim Sully Antiques
01483 579652
Pages 100a, 154al.

Kjaerholm's
+ 45 45 76 56 56
www.kjaerholms.dk
Page 20l.

Kristiina Ratia Designs
+ 1 203 852 0027
Pages 168b, 212r, 213l, 213ar.

Knott Architects
020 7263 8844
www.knottarchitects.co.uk
Pages 206r, 222l.

Laura Bohn Design Associates
+ 1 212 645 3636
Page 70ar.

Lloyd Schwan/Design
+ 1 212 375 0858
lloydschwan@earthlink.net
Pages 10, 15a, 134a, 134bl, 144–45.

Lucy Salem
020 8563 2625
lucyandmarcsalem@hot
mail.com
Page 99bl.

Luigi Rosselli
+ 61 2 9281 1498
Pages 64l, 79bcl.

Lulu Guinness
020 7823 4828
www.luluguinness.com
Page 25r.

McMillen Pynn Architecture L.L.P.
+ 1 208 622 4656
www.sunvalleyachitect.com
Page 151ar.

Maisonette
020 8964 8444
www.maisonette.uk.com
Pages 18, 57br, 86a, 161al.

Malin Iovino Design
020 7252 3542
iovino@btconnect.com
Pages 110–11, 164r.

Marino + Giolito
+ 1 212 675 5737
marino.giolito@rcn.com
Pages 180br, 190b, 199al.

Marisa Tadiotto Cavalli
+ 39 02 36 51 14 49
marisacavalli@hotmail.com
Page 171ar.

Mark Brook Design
020 7221 8106
Page 82c.

Mark Kirkley
01424 812613
Page 195b.

Mary Bright
+ 1 212 677 1970
www.marybright.com
Page 29.

Michael Nathenson Unique Environments
020 7431 6978
www.unique-
environments.co.uk
Pages 75ar, 185ar, 194br.

Miv Watts Design
01328 730557/83
www.wattswishedfor.com
Pages 160a both.

Mona Nerenberg (Bloom)
+ 1 631 725 4680
Page 32b

Moneo Brock Studio
+ 34 91 563 8056
www.moneobrock.com
Pages 16bc, 66b, 70al, 72a, 189ac, 204bl.

Mullman Seidman Architects
+ 1 212 431 0770
www.mullmanseidman.com
Pages 32ar, 67r, 68r, 70bl, 104l, 104–105, 105br, 106r, 131b, 160b, 178l, 186l, 189bl, 192, 194a, 195ar, 203l, 216r, 218 inset, 220r.

Nelly Guyot Décoratrice
+ 33 06 09 25 20 68
Page 46l.

Nico Rensch Architeam
01424 445 885
www.architeam.co.uk
Pages 67l, 84r, 143.

Nicole Fabre
020 7384 3112
Page 100a.

Nigel Smith
020 7278 8802
n-smith@dircon.co.uk
Page 187br.

Orefelt Associates
020 8960 2560
orefelt@msn.com
Pages 186r, 197a, 206al, 210bl, 216l.

Ory Gomez Didier Gomez
+ 33 01 44 30 8823
orygomez@free.fr
Pages 6, 120, 162ar.

Ou Baholyodhin Studio
020 7426 0666
www.ou-b.com
Page 96br.

Paul Collier Architect
+ 33 1 53 72 49 32
paul.collier@architecte.net
Pages 106l, 108bl, 162c.

Paul Daly Design Studio
020 7613 4855
www.pauldaly.com
Pages 15b, 219bl.

Philip Hooper
020 7978 6662
Page 16al.

Reed Creative Services
020 7565 0066
Pages 81br, 141al, 185l.

Retrouvius Reclamation & Design
tel/fax 020 7724 3387
Page 89r.

Roger Oates
01531 632718
www.rogeroates.co.uk
Pages 23ac, 162bl, 163br, 181l.

Sage and Coombe Architects
+ 1 212 226 9600
www.sageandcoombe.com
Pages 118–19.

Sally Storey John Cullen Lighting
020 7371 5400
Pages 81br, 185l.

Sandy Davidson Design
fax + 1 320 659 2107
SandSandD@aol.com
Page 207c.

Sarah Featherstone
Featherstone Associates
020 7490 1212
www.featherstone-
associates.co.uk
Pages 172–73.

Sasha Gibb
01534 863211
home@sashagibb.co.uk
Page 28a.

Schack-Arnott
Danish Classic Moderne
+ 61 3 9525 0250
Page 85br.

Schefer Design
+ 1 212 691 9097
www.scheferdesign.com
Pages 46a, 46br.

Sera Hersham-Loftus
020 7286 5948
Pages 204br, 209r.

Seth Stein
020 8968 8581
www.sethstein.com
*Pages 4c, 82r, 97br,
148l, 196bl.*

Sharland & Lewis
01666 500354
www.sharland&lewis.com
Page 47l.

Sheppard Day Design
020 7821 2002
Pages 69, 115bl, 158.

**Sidnam Petrone Gartner
Architects**
+ 1 212 366 5500
www.spgarchitects.com
Page 184l.

**Simon Colebrook
Douglas Stephen
Partnership**
020 7336 7884
www.dspl.co.uk
Page 58l.

Site Specific
020 7490 3176
www.sitespecificltd.co.uk
Pages 94l, 146.

Stephen Slan A.I.A.
+ 1 323 962 9101
www.viarc.com
Pages 132al, 150bl.

Stephen Turvil Architects
020 8299 6169
info@stephenturvil
architects.com
www.stephenturvil
architects.com
Pages 196a, 214, 214–15.

Steven Learner Studio
+ 1 212 741 8583
www.stevenlearner
studio.com
Pages 77, 130–31b.

Steven Sclaroff, Designer
+ 1 212 691 7814
sclaroff@aol.com
Page 88r.

Stickland Coombe
020 7924 1699
www.sticklandcoombe.com
Pages 42a, 149a both.

The Moderns
+ 1 212 387 8852
www.themoderns.com
Pages 26–27, 95cr.

The Swedish Chair
020 8657 8560
www.theswedishchair.com
Page 224bl.

The Rug Company
020 7229 5148
www.therugcompany.info
Page 170al.

Touch Interior Design
020 7498 6409
*Pages 70br 126br, 127,
158–59.*

Tsao & McKown
+ 1 212 337 3800
fax +1 212 337 0013
Pages 200–201.

Urban Research Lab
020 8709 9060
www.urbanresearch
lab.com
*Pages 122–23, 181r,
196–97a.*

Urban Salon
020 7357 8800
*Pages 12–13, 13al,
90–91, 205l, 225br.*

USE Architects
020 8986 8111
use.arch@virgin.net
Page 119r.

VX design & architecture
020 7370 5496
www.vxdesign.com
*Pages 42b,51, 79bcr,
97ar, 202r.*

**Vanessa Arbuthnott
Fabrics**
www.vanessa
arbuthnott.co.uk
Page 16cl.

Vicente Wolf Associates, Inc.
+ 1 212 465 0590
www.vicentewolf
associates.com
Pages 177, 199ar.

Voon Wong & Benson Saw
020 7587 0116
www.voon-benson.com
*Pages 41al, 78r, 96a,
150r.*

Wallensteen & Co ab
+ 46 8 210151
wallensteen@chello.se
Page 43ar.

William R. Hefner AIA
+ 1 323 931 1365
www.williamhefner.com
Page 207c.

Woodhams Landscape
020 7346 5656
www.woodhams.co.uk
Page 73br.

Woodnotes OY
+ 358 9694 2200
www.woodnotes.fi
*Pages 2–3, 36–37, 40r,
43b.*

Woolf Architects
020 7428 9500
Pages 8–9.

Yves-Claude Design
www.kanso.com
*Pages 68c, 72br, 92–93
both.*

**Yves Halard, Interior
Decoration**
+ 33 1 44 07 14 00
Page 71l.

ZG Design
+ 1 631 537 4454
www.zgdesign.com
Page 180al.

Zynk Design Consultants
020 7721 7444
www.zynkdesign.com
Pages 184r, 205l.

index